MINIMALIST HOUSES
MAISONS MINIMALISTES
MINIMALISTISCHE HÄUSER

MINIMALIST HOUSES
MAISONS MINIMALISTES
MINIMALISTISCHE HÄUSER

EVERGREEN

EVERGREEN is an imprint of

Taschen GmbH

© 2006 TASCHEN GmbH

Hohenzollernring 53, D-50672 Köln

www.taschen.com

Editor Editrice Redakteur:
Simone Schleifer

English translation Traduction anglaise Englische Übersetzung:
Jane Wintle

French translation Traduction française Französische Übersetzung:
Marion Westerhoff

German translation Traduction allemande Deutsche Übersetzung:
Susanne Engler

Proof reading Relecture Korrektur:
Matthew Clarke, Marie-Pierre Santamarina, Martin Rolshoven

Art director Direction artistique Art Direktor:
Mireia Casanovas Soley

Graphic design and layout Mise en page et maquette Graphische Gestaltung und Layout:
Diego González

Printed by Imprimé par Gedruckt durch:
Gráficas Toledo, Spain

ISBN: 3-8228-5145-0

Contents Index Inhalt

The architect Ludwig Mies van der Rohe adopted the motto "Less is more" to describe his aesthetic tactics of flattening and emphasizing the building's frame, eliminating interior walls, adopting an open plan, and reducing the structure to a strong yet transparent and elegant skin. In contrast, the designer Buckminster Fuller, adopted a similar saying, "Doing more with less", but his concerns were more oriented towards technology and engineering than aesthetics. In both cases, they have been considered practitioners of "minimalist architecture", at times with caution and at times with certain conviction. This term has been used to describe the work of numerous architects from across the world who have based their work on a reduction in expressive media, a rediscovery of the value of empty space and a radical elimination of everything that does not coincide with a program. It is often associated with minimalist interior design, which also adopts the approach of extreme simplicity and formal purity.

Nowadays, in the construction of minimalist houses the main goal is to find modes of design that go further than a simple denunciation of complexity, and begin to move towards imbuing space with a modest sense of spirituality, clarity, and harmony. These designs have begun to move out of closed architectural circles and are becoming increasingly in more accessible to the general public. This is especially true to residential design, where those who are looking to build their own houses, or update their existing ones, can find an endless source of inspiration from the houses being designed by contemporary minimalist architects.

Some of the projects shown in this book involve highly complex systems of engineering and construction, while others employ simple techniques that result in efficient and aesthetic designs. Still others explore the numerous possibilities of "building green" in order to reduce the intake of energy and respect the surrounding environment. The idea of minimalism can be interpreted in a diverse number of ways and can utilize a wide range of expressive media. The exploration of this style shows the endless number of possibilities still offered by this elegant and historical style. "Minimalist Houses" offers an extensive collection of contemporary houses designed by renowned architects that provide the architect, homeowner, and avid reader alike with a wealth of ideas for maximizing the potential of a new residence and making the most of the space available. It takes its inspiration from the most recently completed homes from around the world.

La devise « moins est plus » de l'architecte Ludwig Mies van der Rohe, résume sa technique esthétique de nivelage et d'exaltation de la structure de l'édifice : éliminer les cloisons intérieures pour adopter un plan ouvert et réduire le rôle structural à une élégante toiture, à la fois résistante et transparente. A l'inverse de ce dernier, Buckminster Fuller, designer et architecte, dont la devise assez semblable était « faire plus avec moins », a davantage centré ses préoccupations sur la technologie et l'ingénierie que sur l'esthétique. Ces deux tendances ont toutefois un dénominateur commun puisque l'une et l'autre sont qualifiées d' « architecture minimaliste ». Cette appellation, employée tantôt avec prudence, tantôt avec une conviction absolue, décrit la conception architecturale de nombre d'architectes du monde entier dont l'oeuvre se base sur une réduction des moyens d'expression, une redécouverte de la valeur de l'espace vide et une élimination radicale de tout ce qui est superflu face à programme donné. Ce terme est fréquemment associé au design minimaliste d'intérieurs, également axé sur l'extrême sobriété et la perfection des formes.

Aujourd'hui, l'objectif essentiel, dans la construction d'habitations minimalistes, est de créer des formes de design, qui, au-delà d'une simple dénonciation de la complexité, visent à imprégner l'espace d'une sensation purement spirituelle, clair et harmonieuse. Ces designs commencent à sortir des cercles architecturaux fermés, dont ils faisaient partie par le passé, pour devenir de plus en plus accessibles. Ceci est particulièrement vrai du design résidentiel où, les personnes aspirant à construire leur propre demeure ou à la remodeler, peuvent trouver une source inépuisable d'inspiration auprès de nombreuses réalisations d'architectes minimalistes contemporains.

Dans cet ouvrage, certains projets employant des systèmes d'ingénierie et de construction d'une grande complexité, côtoient ceux qui utilisent des techniques plus simples pour réussir des designs efficaces et esthétiques. D'autres vont au-delà, en explorant les nombreuses alternatives offertes par la « construction écologique » pour réduire la consommation d'énergie et respecter l'environnement naturel. Le minimalisme s'interprète de diverses façons et offre un large éventail de moyens d'expression. Style à l'élégance légendaire, il offre des possibilités infinies. « Maisons minimalistes » propose une large sélection d'habitations contemporaines. Conçues par des architectes de renom qui proposent au maître d'oeuvre, propriétaire ou lecteur une foule d'idées pour maximaliser le potentiel et l'espace disponible d'une nouvelle habitation, ces maisons minimalistes récentes, issues du monde entier, sont une merveilleuse source d'inspiration.

Der Architekt Ludwig Mies van der Rohe benutzte das Motto „weniger ist mehr", das seine ästhetische Technik erklärt, um die Struktur eines Gebäudes zu ebnen und zu unterstreichen. Im Gegensatz dazu übernahm der Architekt und Designer Buckminster Fuller einen ähnlichen Leitgedanken, „mit weniger mehr machen", fokussierte dabei jedoch mehr auf die Technologie und das Ingenieurwesen als auf die Ästhetik. In beiden Fällen handelt es sich um „minimalistische Architektur". Dieser Ausdruck, der manchmal mit Bedachtsamkeit und manchmal mit vollster Überzeugung benutzt wird, beschreibt Werke zahlreicher Architekten auf der ganzen Welt, die ihre Arbeit auf eine Reduktion der Ausdrucksmittel, ein Neuentdecken des Wertes des leeren Raums und eine radikale Eliminierung von allem, was nicht den Wohnfunktionen dient, basieren.

Heutzutage ist es das wichtigste Ziel bei der Errichtung von minimalistischen Häusern, Formen der Gestaltung zu finden, die über einen einfachen Verzicht auf die Komplexität hinausgehen und die darauf hinzielen, dem Raum einen zurückhaltenden Eindruck von Spiritualität, Klarheit und Harmonie zu verleihen. Diese Art der Gestaltung findet man heutzutage nicht mehr nur innerhalb eines geschlossenen Kreises von Architekten, wie dies in der Vergangenheit der Fall war, sondern sie wird für jeden zugänglich. Bei einigen der Häuser, die in diesem Buch vorgestellt werden, sind sehr komplexe Ingenieurstechniken und Konstruktionssysteme eingesetzt worden, während für andere wiederum einfache Techniken angewandt wurden, durch die effiziente und ästhetische Entwürfe entstanden sind. Andere gehen noch einen Schritt weiter und erforschen die immer größer werdenden Möglichkeiten für eine ökologische Bauweise, um den Energieverbrauch zu mindern und die Umgebung zu respektieren.

Die Idee des Minimalismus kann auf viele verschiedene Weisen interpretiert und es können sehr viele verschiedene Ausdrucksmittel angewendet werden. Wenn man diese Idee näher betrachtet, offenbaren sich die unzähligen Möglichkeiten, die dieser elegante und historische Stil zu bieten hat. „Minimalistische Häuser" zeigt eine große Auswahl an zeitgemäßen Behausungen, die von berühmten Architekten entworfen wurden und sowohl dem Architekten als auch dem Hauseigentümer, als begeistertem Leser, eine Unmenge an Ideen geben, um die Möglichkeiten einer neuen Wohnung lauszureizen und den vorhandenen Platz maximal auszunutzen. Dazu inspirieren einige dieser Häuser im minimalistischen Stil, die in der letzten Zeit auf der ganzen Welt entstanden.

Asencio House

Maison Asencio

Haus Asencio

The bright luminosity of Cadiz is the main design element in this house, which is inspired by the typical Andalusian house and devised so that light pours in diagonally and becomes the unifying element in the project. The house is on various levels so that the carefully designed interior space benefits from an imaginative lighting scheme. Strategically placed skylights show how a single light source can illuminate different parts of a house. Communal areas are separated from the private spaces: the front of the building holds the communal areas, the dining room and library, whilst the rear of the building contains bedrooms and bathrooms. The rectangular doors have been replaced by large square glass doorways that frame the views of the pine woods and golf course in front of the house.

La lumière intense de Cadiz est l'élément dominant du design de cette habitation, qui s'inspire des maisons typiquement andalouses et dont la conception fait que la lumière la traverse en diagonal, devenant l'élément unificateur du projet. Forte de ses divers niveaux, la maison peut exploiter l'espace intérieur, soigneusement planifié, pour concevoir un système d'éclairage original. La disposition stratégique des lucarnes montre qu'une seule source de lumière peut éclairer différentes zones de l'habitation. Les espaces communs et privés sont séparés : la partie avant de l'habitation héberge les zones communes, la salle à manger et la bibliothèque, tandis que la partie arrière accueille les chambres à coucher et les salles de bains. Les portes rectangulaires cèdent la place aux grandes portes carrées de verre qui encadrent les vues sur la pinède du golf situé en face de la demeure.

Das intensive Licht von Cadiz ist das Hauptgestaltungselement für dieses Haus, das von den typischen andalusischen Häusern inspiriert ist. Es ist so angelegt, dass das Licht diagonal das Haus durchquert und es vereinheitlicht. Das Gebäude hat verschiedene Ebenen, so dass der sorgfältig geplante Innenraum benutzt werden kann, um ein originelles Beleuchtungssystem zu schaffen. Die strategische Anordnung der Dachfenster beweist, dass man mit einer einzigen Lichtquelle verschiedene Bereiche des Hauses beleuchten kann. Die Gemeinschaftsräume sind von den privaten Räumen getrennt. Im vorderen Bereich des Hauses liegen die gemeinsamen Räume, das Speisezimmer und die Bibliothek und im hinteren Teil die Schlafzimmer und Badezimmer. Die rechteckigen Türen wurden durch große quadratische Glastüren ersetzt, die den Blick auf den Pinienwald des Golfplatzes gegenüber des Hauses einrahmen.

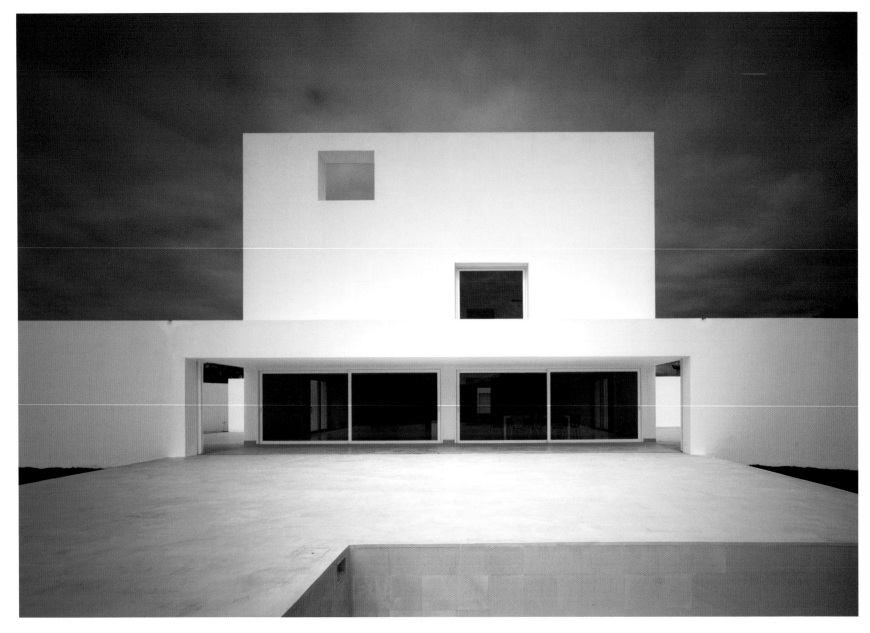

Large square glass doors frame the views of the pine trees by the golf links opposite the house.

De grandes portes carrées de verre encadrent les vues sur la pinède du golf situé en face de la maison.

Große quadratische Glastüren umrahmen den Blick auf den Pinienwald des Golfplatzes gegenüber dem Haus.

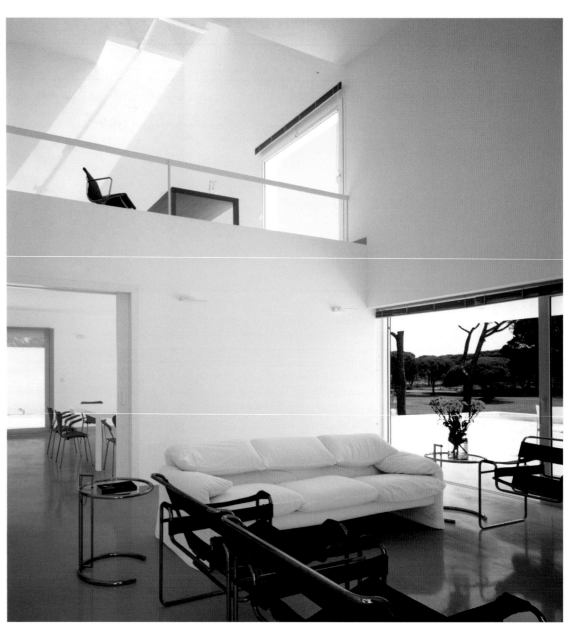

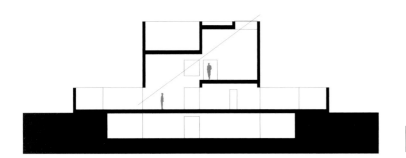

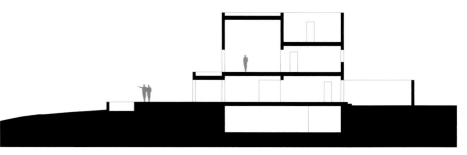

› Sections Sections Schnitte

The bedrooms and bathrooms are located in the rear of the house.

La partie arrière accueille les chambres à coucher et les salles de bain.

Im hinteren Teil der Wohnung liegen die Schlafzimmer und Bäder.

The kitchen is designed with a simple layout and clean lines.

La cuisine se définit par des lignes droites et par un concept sobre et simplifié.

Die Küche zeichnet sich durch die geraden Linien und das einfache Konzept aus.

Residence in Monte Atros

Maison à Monte Atros

Residenz in Monte Atros

This building was built 18 ft from the street, and 10 ft from the other boundaries of the plot, to conform with the strict city planning regulations and also create a transitional space between the public and private areas. The composition achieves privacy by means of a series of walls screening an outside garden and a terrace, directly accessible from the house. The house is on three levels: the bedrooms are located on the third floor, the salon and communal areas on the second and the service areas on the ground floor. The patio allows daylight to enter at ground level, whilst skylights and windows placed at strategic heights and positions also permit natural light to enter the home. The white walls, stone floors and comfortable furniture set off the attractive decorative features and color scheme.

Cet édifice, construit à cinq mètres de la rue et à trois mètres des autres limites de la propriété, conformément aux normes d'urbanisme, crée en même temps une aire de transition entre le public et le privé. La structure façonne un univers intime grâce à une série de murs masquant un jardin extérieur et une terrasse communiquant directement avec les espaces intérieurs. La maison s'articule autour de trois niveaux : les chambres à coucher sont situées au troisième étage, le salon et les aires communes au deuxième, et les aires de service au sous-sol. Grâce au patio, la lumière pénètre le sous-sol, tandis que les lucarnes et les fenêtres de différentes tailles, hauteurs et composition inondent l'habitation de lumière. Les murs blancs, les sols de pierre et le confortable mobilier servent de toile de fond pour mettre en valeur les tons choisis et les objets décoratifs insolites.

Dieses Haus steht fünf Meter von der Straße und drei Meter von den anderen Grundstücksgrenzen entfernt, so wie es die strengen Bauvorschriften vorschreiben. So entstand ein Durchgang zwischen dem öffentlichen Bereich und dem privaten. Die Struktur schafft mittels einer Reihe von Mauern, die den direkt mit dem Inneren verbundenen Garten und eine Terrasse verbergen, Privatsphäre. Das Haus besteht aus drei Ebenen: die Schlafzimmer befinden sich in der 2. Etage, das Wohnzimmer und die gemeinsamen Bereiche in der ersten und die funktionellen Räume im Erdgeschoss. Durch den Hof fällt Licht in das Erdgeschoss, während die anderen Räume ihr Tageslicht durch Dachfenster und andere Fenster verschiedener Größe, Höhe und Kompositionen erhalten. Die weißen Wände, der Boden aus Naturstein und die komfortablen Möbel bilden den Hintergrund, vor dem kontrastreiche Farbtöne und interessante Dekorationsobjekte gezeigt werden.

The white walls, stone floors and comfortable furniture set off the attractive decorative features and color scheme.

Les murs blancs, les sols de pierre et le confortable mobilier servent de toile de fond pour exalter les tons choisis et les objets décoratifs insolites.

Die weißen Wände, der Boden aus Naturstein und die komfortablen Möbel bilden den Hintergrund, vor dem kontrastreiche Farbtöne und interessante Dekorationsobjekte gezeigt werden.

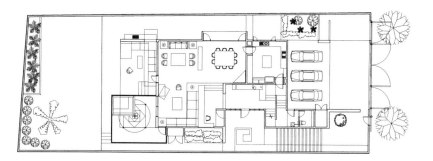

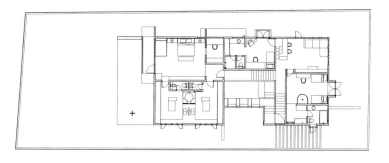

› Ground floor   Rez-de-chaussée   Erdgeschoss

› First floor   Premier étage   Erstes Obergeschoss

Mesh Design
La maille
Die Masche

Located in a residential quarter of western Tokyo, this six-home complex was designed to rediscover the cityscape by using an unusual configuration and a simple architectural language expressed through linear volumes. In this T-shaped composition, constructed space and untouched areas create an interactive network, unified by materials and open spaces. Its cubic form sought to maintain a certain degree of continuity with the neighborhood, without building or organizing the interiors, by reinterpreting the traditional Japanese "engawa". The reflective finish of the floors contrasts with the dark facade, adding a dramatic quality to the transition between the inner and outer environments. The architect used the "engawa" concept to stress union, rather than rupture, between the interior of the home and the exterior.

Situé dans une zone résidentielle à l'ouest de Tokyo, ce complexe de six habitations a été conçu pour redécouvrir le paysage urbain grâce à une configuration atypique et un langage architectural simple aux volumes linéaires. La composition en T crée une interaction unique entre l'espace construit et non construit, en utilisant les matériaux et les vides comme éléments unificateurs. Le volume cubique de cette configuration est conçu pour garder une certaine homogénéité avec le quartier voisin sans construire ni organiser les intérieurs en réinterprétant la traditionnelle « engawa » japonaise. Le fini réfléchissant des sols génère une luminosité qui contraste avec l'allure sombre de la façade, exaltant la transition graduelle entre l'intérieur et l'extérieur. Conçu comme l'espace d'une maison japonaise qui sépare l'extérieur de l'intérieur, l'architecte utilise ici le concept de « engawa » pour exprimer l'union plus que la séparation.

Dieser Wohnkomplex mit sechs Wohnungen liegt in einem Wohnviertel im Westen Tokios. Man wollte die Stadtlandschaft durch eine untypische Gestaltung und eine einfache architektonische Sprache, die sich in lineare Formen umsetzt, neu entdecken. Das Gebäude hat die Form eines T's, so dass eine einzigartige Wechselwirkung zwischen dem bebauten und dem unbebauten Raum entsteht, wobei die Materie und die Leerräume als vereinende Elemente benutzt werden. Man entschied sich für die Würfelform, um eine gewisse Kontinuität zum benachbarten, unbebauten Grundstück zu schaffen. Die Räume sind eine Neuinterpretation des traditionellen, japanischen „Engawa". Die spiegelnden Böden sorgen für viel Helligkeit, die zu den dunklen Fassaden im Kontrast steht. Dadurch wird der allmähliche Übergang von innen nach außen unterstrichen. Der Architekt benutzte bei der Gestaltung des Raumes das Konzept „Engawa", das mehr die Verbindung als die Trennung ausdrücken soll.

Black metal panels on the main facade contrast with large glazed areas and a light, white volume next to the main building.

Sur la façade on a utilisé des panneaux noirs en métal combinés à de grandes baies vitrées et un volume léger et blanc en face de l'édifice principal.

An der Fassade wurden schwarze Metallpaneele und große Glasfenster mit einer leichten weißen Form kombiniert, die dem Hauptgebäude gegenübergestellt wird.

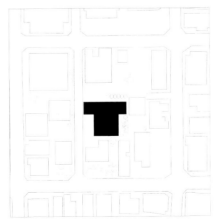

› Location plan   Plan de situation   Umgebungsplan

› Ground floor Rez-de-chaussée Erdgeschoss

› First floor Premier étage Erstes Obergeschoss

› Second floor Deuxième étage Zweites Obergeschoss

House in Alenquer

Maison à Alenquer

Haus in Alenquer

The white geometrical volumes around the swimming pool are the focus of this project, which developed out of the perimeter walls of a ruined house. The ambiguity of the contours produced by the volumes creates a dynamic relationship between the inside and outside spaces. The wooden walkway connecting the independent volumes confers a feeling of privacy on the home. The openings in the walls frame fragments of the green countryside. The clearly defined interior constantly communicates with the exterior through the large, floor-to-ceiling windows.

Les volumes blancs aux formes géométriques, répartis autour de la piscine, constituent l'essence même de ce projet, conçu à partir des murs d'enceinte d'une maison en ruine. L'ambiguïté des limites tracées par les volumes crée une relation dynamique entre les espaces intérieurs et extérieurs. La passerelle en bois qui relie les volumes indépendants confère à l'habitation l'ambiance d'un petit univers privé. Les ouvertures dans les murs encadrent des fragments de verdure du paysage. Les intérieurs, clairement définis, communiquent constamment avec l'extérieur grâce à de grandes baies vitrées, allant du sol au plafond.

Dieses Gebäude besteht aus weißen geometrischen Formen, die einen Swimmingpool umgeben. Ausgangspunkt der Planung waren die Außenwände eines abgerissenen Hauses. Die Doppeldeutigkeit der von den Formen geschaffenen Grenzen lässt eine dynamische Beziehung zwischen den Räumen außen und innen entstehen. Der Laufsteg aus Holz, der zwei unabhängige Blöcke miteinander verbindet, lässt das Haus wie einen kleinen, privaten Wohnkomplex wirken. Maueröffnungen umrahmen den Blick auf die grüne Landschaft der Umgebung. Die klar definierten Innenräume stehen durch vom Boden bis zur Decke reichende Fenster ständig mit der äußeren Umgebung in Verbindung.

The openings in the walls frame fragments of the green countryside.

Les ouvertures des murs se métamorphosent en cadres qui capturent la verdure du paysage extérieur.

Die Öffnungen in den Mauern werden zu Rahmen, die die Landschaft der Umgebung einfangen.

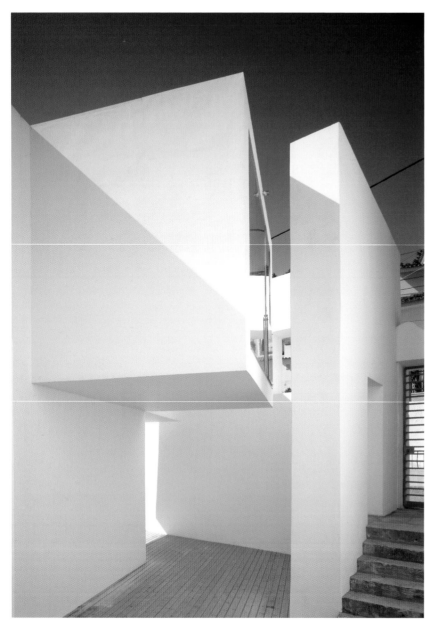

› Sections Sections Schnitte

› Sections Sections Schnitte

Altair

Architects at Engelenmoore studio were faced with the challenge of adding a new structure to this complex and creating a variety of new, flexible spaces. The sixteen-floor apartment block was designed as a slim, rectangular volume raised on a podium, aligned along an east-west axis, with most of the homes facing north. Due to the fact that the property is located over a four-lane traffic tunnel, the construction was subjected to unusual structural limitations and its parking facilities were curtailed. These homes take maximum advantage of their placement and capacity for natural ventilation, with deep cantilevered balconies and aluminum exterior shutters, eliminating the need for air-conditioning. On the outside, the combined effect of the balconies, horizontal and vertical brise-soleil sunscreens, unassuming concrete surfaces and blue and black lift shafts bestows texture and rhythm on the overall structure.

Les architectes de l'étude Engelenmoore ont été placés devant le défi d'adapter une nouvelle structure à ce complexe et de créer des espaces flexibles et variés. La tour d'appartements, à 16 niveaux, située sur le podium, est conçue comme un bloc étroit et rectiligne d'est à ouest permettant à la majorité des habitations d'être tournées vers le nord. Situé au-dessus d'un tunnel routier à quatre voies, l'édifice a été soumis à des restrictions inhabituelles quant à la structure et à l'attribution de zone de parking. Les habitations, conçues pour bénéficier au maximum de l'orientation et de la ventilation naturelle, sont équipées de profonds balcons en encorbellement et de persiennes extérieures en aluminium, permettant de se passer de climatisation. A l'extérieur, l'ensemble des balcons, les brise-soleil horizontaux et verticaux, la sobriété des surfaces en béton et les cages d'ascenseur bleu et blanc créent une structure du plus bel effet, parfaitement agencée.

Die Architekten des Studios Engelenmoore sollten eine neue Struktur an einen bereits existierenden Gebäudekomplex anpassen und vielseitig nutzbare Räume schaffen. Das sechzehnstöckige Wohnhaus steht auf einem Podium und wurde als schmaler, geradliniger Wohnungsblock entworfen, der von Osten nach Westen verläuft, so dass die meisten Wohnungen nach Norden liegen. Er steht über einem vierspurigen Verkehrstunnel, so dass es sehr schwierig war, hier eine Struktur und einen Parkplatz zu schaffen. Die Wohnungen wurden so entworfen, dass ihre Ausrichtung maximal ausgenutzt wird und die Belüftung ausreichend ist. Sie haben tiefe und hervorspringende Balkone sowie Aluminiumjalousien, die ausreichend vor Sonne schützen, so dass man keine Klimaanlage braucht. Die Kombination von Balkonen, waagerechten und senkrechten Brise-soleils, schlichten Flächen aus weißem Zement an der Fassade und die blau-schwarzen Hohlräume des Fahrstuhls schaffen eine interessante Struktur und Gliederung.

This façade, with balconies that capture sunlight both horizontally and vertically, reflects light, giving an overall impression of high-quality architecture.

La façade, dont les balcons captent la lumière du soleil qui entre horizontalement et verticalement, reflète la lumière, renvoyant l'image d'une architecture de haut niveau.

Die Fassade, deren Balkone das Sonnenlicht, das waagerecht und senkrecht einfällt, auffangen, reflektiert das Licht und lässt das Gebäude sehr edel wirken.

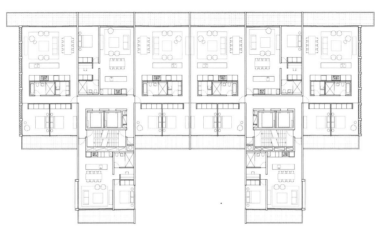

› Plan Plan Grundriss

Two houses in Oropesa del Mar

Deux maisons à Oropesa del Mar

Zwei Häuser in Oropesa del Mar

This project comprised two summer houses on a 3,200-sq.-ft plot. Both houses are symmetrical, with the kitchen and dining room on the first floor and two bedrooms and a bathroom upstairs. The basement, toilets and large ground-floor patio are shared. An adjustable wooden sunscreen (which can be transformed into a delightful pergola) protects the patio, which in turn is both a connecting area and a place to serve meals in the summer. In this configuration, one of the prism's surfaces is removed, transforming the upstairs gallery into a balcony protected from the sun's rays by the lattice covering the ceiling and walls. The building is raised at one end to adapt to the terrain and mantain prism shape. A platform resting on a vertical wall forms a courtyard beneath the house, which can also be used as a carport.

Ce projet prévoit la construction de deux maisons d'été sur une parcelle de 300 m². Les habitations sont symétriques : la cuisine et la salle à manger sont situées au rez-de-chaussée, avec deux chambres et une salle de bain à l'étage supérieur. Les deux maisons partagent les toilettes du sous sol et un grand patio au rez-de-chaussée. Le patio est protégé du soleil grâce à un caillebotis de bois qui peut pivoter pour se transformer en charmante pergola, servant en même temps, de zone de connexion et de lieu pour prendre ses repas en été. Cette configuration élimine un mur du prisme, convertissant la galerie supérieure en un balcon, protégé du soleil par le caillebotis, qui prolonge les murs et sert de membrane de protection solaire. Pour s'adapter au terrain et maintenir la forme de prisme, le bloc s'élève sur un côté. Une plateforme, reposant sur un mur vertical, crée un patio sous la maison, utilisable également comme parking.

Auf einem 300 m² großen Grundstück ließen sich zwei Brüder zwei Sommerhäuser errichten. Die Häuser sind symmetrisch, die Küche und das Speisezimmer liegen im Erdgeschoss, die Schlafzimmer und das Bad im Obergeschoss. Die beiden Häuser haben gemeinsame Badezimmer im Untergeschoss und einen großen Innenhof im Erdgeschoss. Der Hof wird durch ein Holzgeflecht vor der Sonne geschützt, das zu einer wunderschönen Pergola werden kann, die gleichzeitig als Esszimmer für den Sommer dient. Bei dieser Anordnung fehlt eine Wand des Prismas und die obere Galerie wird zu einem Balkon, der durch das Holzgeflecht vor der Sonne geschützt wird. Das Gebäude wurde an einer Seite angehoben um sich dem Gelände anzupassen und die Form des Primas zu erhalten. Eine Plattform, die auf einer senkrechten Mauer ruht, lässt einen Hof unter dem Haus entstehen, der auch zum Parken benutzt werden kann.

The combination of wood and concrete gives a special rhythm to the building's facades.

L'association de matériaux comme le bois et le béton confère un rythme spécial à toutes les façades de l'édifice.

Die Kombination von Materialien wie Holz und Beton markiert den Rhythmus der Fassaden des gesamten Gebäudes.

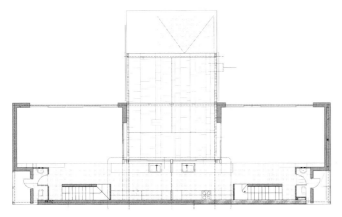

› Ground floor Rez-de-chaussée Erdgeschoss

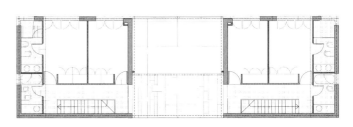

› First floor Premier étage Erstes Obergeschoss

Apartments in Sabadell

Appartements à Sabadell

Wohnungen in Sabadell

This project comprises sixteen homes, arranged in a rectangular block of wood and stone. The three-story building, composed of two volumes linked by an inner patio to circulation areas, is remarkable for the clean-cut sobriety of its lines. Of its three facades, the two facing the street are built entirely of wood and stone, while the third, fully glazed facade overlooking the patio is finished in wood and aluminium strips, echoing the interior layout of the apartments inside. In all, the building contains twelve duplex and four single-level apartments, each one accessed from the interior patio. The main facade is chiefly of stone; the windows have sliding wooden shutters and aluminium frames, whose darker colours underline the division between each story. Indirect floor lighting and skylights bring pleasant, filtered light to all the communal spaces.

Le projet accueille seize habitations disposées en un bloc rectangulaire constitué de pierres et de bois. L'édifice de trois étages est composé de deux volumes reliés aux zones de circulation par le biais d'un patio intérieur, qui se distingue par son aspect linéaire et sobre. Trois façades composent l'édifice : deux d'entre elles, utilisant la pierre et le bois, sont tournées vers la rue et la troisième, s'ouvrant sur le patio, est réalisée en verre, liteaux de bois et tiges d'aluminium qui tracent la composition intérieure des appartements. Il y a douze duplex et quatre habitations simples, toutes accessibles depuis le patio intérieur. La façade, principalement réalisée en pierre, intègre également des contre-fenêtres coulissantes en bois aux cadres d'aluminium, dont la couleur plus sombre différencie les appartements. L'éclairage au sol indirect et les lucarnes dispensent une lumière douce, tamisée, créant un environnement agréable dans les espaces communs.

Dieses Gebäude beherbergt sechzehn Wohnungen, die in einem rechteckigen Block aus Stein und Holz untergebracht sind. Das dreistöckige Gebäude besteht aus zwei Teilen, die in den Durchgangsbereichen durch einen linearen und schlichten Innenhof vereint sind. Das Gebäude hat drei Fassaden, zwei davon liegen zur Straße und sind aus Naturstein und Holz, die dritte Fassade liegt zum Innenhof und ist aus Glas, Holzleisten und Aluminiumstreifen, die eine Komposition bilden, die das Innere der Wohnungen dekoriert. In dem Gebäude gibt es zwölf zweistöckige und vier Wohnungen ohne Etagen, in die man durch den Innenhof gelangt. Die Fassade besteht hauptsächlich aus Naturstein, die Fensterläden sind aus Holz und die Fensterrahmen aus Aluminium, wobei deren dunklere Farbe die verschiedenen Etagen hervorhebt. Die indirekte Beleuchtung im Boden und die Dachfenster sorgen für ein leicht diffuses Licht, das in den gemeinsamen Bereichen eine sehr angenehme Atmosphäre schafft.

The wooden panels on the facade can be drawn into a fully closed position to create an abstract, minimalist look.

Les panneaux de bois de la façade peuvent être fermés entièrement pour créer un édifice de forme abstraite et minimaliste.

Die Holzplatten an der Fassade können vollständig geschlossen werden, um eine abstrakte und minimalistische Form zu schaffen.

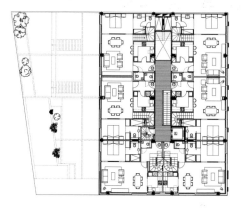

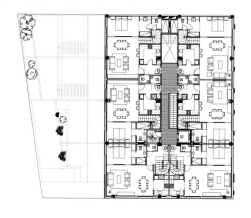

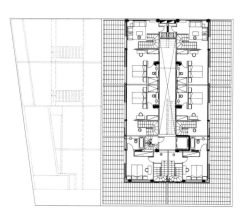

› Plans Plans Grundrisse

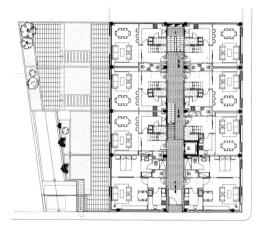

› Ground floor Rez-de-chaussée Erdgeschoss

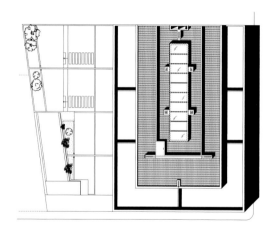

› Roof plan Plan du toit Dachgeschoss

Teng House

Maison Teng

Haus Teng

The main focus of this project—a narrow three-story house with no outside views, separated from the neighbouring house by a dividing wall—was the interior of the property. A skylight was put into the center of the house to provide natural light, as well as views of the different levels. This skylight combines with other light sources to bring diffuse lighting to the first floor. The structure is composed of two blocks on three different levels, separated by another skylight. Glass and steel bridges span the second and third levels, connecting the rear and front parts of the house. Inside, the surfaces and empty spaces interact with light to create multiple spatial experiences, conveying a sense of serenity and perfect minimalist construction.

Le projet, concernant cette étroite maison de trois étages, séparée d'une autre par un mur mitoyen et dépourvue de vues sur l'extérieur, est axé sur l'intérieur. Le centre de la structure comporte un puits de lumière qui baigne l'espace de lumière zénithale et confère des vues aux différents étages. La lucarne et des sources de lumière additionnelles dispensent au premier étage un éclairage diffus. La structure se compose de deux blocs sur trois hauteurs séparées par un autre puits de lumière. Les passerelles d'acier et de verre se croisent dans le vide aux deuxième et troisième étages, reliant l'avant à l'arrière de la maison. L'intérieur, les superficies et les renfoncements en interaction avec la lumière configurent diverses expériences spatiales et transmettent une impression de sérénité et de minimalisme poussés à la perfection.

Bei der Gestaltung dieses schmalen, dreistöckigen Hauses – ein Reihenhaus, von dem man keinen besonders schönen Blick nach draußen hat – konzentrierte man sich auf die Innenräume. Im Zentrum der Struktur wurde ein Dachfenster geschaffen, durch das von oben Licht einfällt sowie Einblicke in die verschiedenen Stockwerke ermöglicht. Durch das Dachfenster und zusätzliche Lichtquellen wird der erste Stock in ein diffuses Licht getaucht. Die Struktur besteht aus zwei Blöcken mit drei Ebenen, die durch eine Lichtsäule getrennt sind. Die Brücken aus Stahl und Glas, die auf der zweiten und dritten Ebene den leeren Raum überspannen, verbinden den hinteren und den vorderen Teil des Hauses. Durch die Wechselwirkung zwischen den Flächen und den Hohlräumen mit dem Licht entstehen viele verschiedene räumliche Eindrücke. Die Wohnumgebung wirkt gelassen und perfekt minimalistisch.

A centrally placed skylight provides overhead light and views of the different levels.

Le coeur de la structure est doté d'une lucarne qui baigne l'espace de lumière zénithale et procure des vues aux différents étages.

Im Zentrum der Struktur wurde ein Dachfenster geschaffen, durch das von oben Licht einfällt. Man blickt auf die verschiedenen Stockwerke.

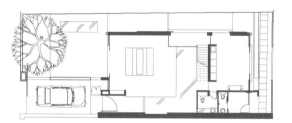

› **Ground floor** Rez-de-chaussée Erdgeschoss

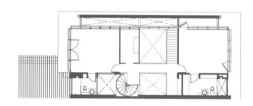

› **First floor** Premier étage Erstes Obergeschoss

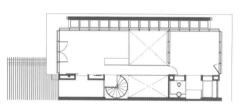

› **Second floor** Deuxième étage Zweites Obergeschoss

Kings Lane

This complex takes up an entire block, and includes two pre-existing, three-storey commercial buildings with a new atrium structure between them, and a newly-built residential unit on the rooftops. The homes on the upper levels occupy a slaping pavilion in a light metal cladding, set back from the commercial building's edges. The three-bedroom homes are designed on two levels in order to benefit from a greater amount of daylight in winter and good views of the cityscape. The large north-facing terraces are annexed to the living rooms, secluded from the adjacent patios by translucent white glass partitions. The latticed aluminum pergolas provide shelter from the sun. Stairwells and corridors provide plenty of natural ventilation, and skylights in the bathrooms and over the stairs allow light into the upper areas.

Ce complexe mixte comprend tout un pâté de maisons et deux édifices commerciaux déjà existants de trois étages, avec une nouvelle structure d'atrium entre eux et un nouvel élément résidentiel inclus dans la toiture des édifices. Les habitations supérieures sont situées dans un pavillon incliné, doté d'un revêtement métallique léger, éloigné des clôtures des édifices commerciaux. Les habitations de trois chambres à coucher ont une double hauteur pour maximaliser l'entrée de la lumière en hiver et offrir une vue panoramique sur l'horizon urbain. Les grands patios orientés Nord, partent des zones de séjour et se protégent des patios contiguë grâce à des murs en verre blanc translucide. Les toitures en pergola, dotées de persiennes d'aluminium ajustables, dispensent de l'ombre et protègent du soleil. Les escaliers et les couloirs dispensent la ventilation nécessaire et les lucarnes, situées dans les salles de bains et au-dessus des escaliers, filtrent la lumière dans la partie supérieure des volumes.

Dieser Gebäudekomplex mit gemischter Nutzung steht auf einem Grundstück, auf dem sich bereits zwei dreistöckige Geschäftshäuser, eine neue Struktur, die ein Atrium zwischen diesen Häusern bildet, und ein neuer Wohnkomplex auf den Dächern der Gebäude befinden. Die höher liegenden Wohnungen befinden sich in einem geneigten Pavillon, der mit Leichtmetall verkleidet ist, wobei sie etwas von den Brüstungen der Geschäftsgebäude entfernt sind. Die Wohnungen mit drei Schlafzimmern haben doppelte Höhe, so dass im Winter sehr viel Tageslicht einfällt und man einen schönen Blick auf die städtische Umgebung hat. Die großen Höfe in Nordrichtung gehen von den Wohnzimmern aus und werden von den angrenzenden Höfen mit Wänden aus weißem, lichtdurchlässigem Glas geschützt. Die Dächer der Pergolas, mit einer einstellbaren Aluminiumjalousie, schützen vor der Sonne. Die Treppen und Flure sorgen für ausreichende Belüftung und die Dachfenster in den Bädern und über den Treppen filtern das Licht in den oberen Etagen.

The ground floor is a single, uninterrupted space: movable panels provide the sole means to create interior partitions.

Le rez-de-chaussée est un espace entièrement ouvert : seuls des panneaux amovibles en distribuent les différentes zones.

Das Erdgeschoss ist ein völlig offener Raum, nur die beweglichen Paneele unterteilen die verschiedenen Bereiche.

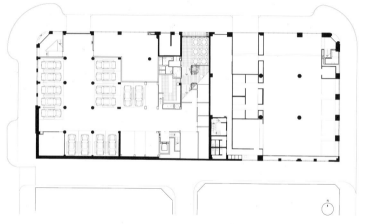

› Ground floor Rez-de-chaussée Erdgeschoss

Clontarf

The challenge in this project was to reconcile the house's new placement with the views enjoyed by the opposite ends of the site. The architectural solution lay in two-level spaces, glass walls and ample open-plan spaces that allow light to enter inside. Notwithstanding the relatively reduced dimensions of the site, the house offers a variety of open-air spaces that satisfy the desire for a contemporary life style. By taking advantage of exterior spaces—often ignored in design—, functional and comfortable living spaces can be created, especially in warm weather. During the winter months, the owners can enjoy the northern part of the home, which receives direct sunlight. The terrace on the south side has panoramic views of the harbor.

Dans ce projet, le nouveau défi à relever était de concilier la nouvelle orientation de la maison avec les vues offertes aux extrémités opposées du terrain. La solution architecturale a été de créer des espaces de double hauteur, des murs de verre et de larges espaces de vie ouverts inondant l'intérieur de lumière. Malgré les dimensions relativement réduites du terrain, l'habitation offre une diversité d'espaces à ciel ouvert répondant parfaitement aux exigences du style de vie contemporain. L'exploitation de l'espace extérieur, souvent ignorée par le design, peut créer des zones très utiles et confortables, surtout sous des climats tempérés. En hiver, les propriétaires peuvent profiter de la zone nord, ensoleillée, de l'habitation. Sur le côté sud, la terrasse, offre une vue panoramique sur le port.

Die Herausforderung bei dieser Planung war es, die neue Ausrichtung des Hauses mit dem Blick in Einklang zu bringen, den man von den beiden Enden des Grundstücks hat. Die architektonische Lösung besteht in einem Raum doppelter Höhe mit verglasten Wänden und weiten, offenen und sehr hellen Räumen. Obwohl das Grundstück relativ klein ist, verfügt das Haus über eine Reihe von Räumen im Freien, die die Anforderungen an eine zeitgenössische Wohnumgebung erfüllen. Oft wird der Außenbereich bei der Planung nicht besonders berücksichtigt, obwohl durch die Einbeziehung der nicht bebauten Flächen, insbesondere in gemäßigten Klimazonen, sehr nützliche und komfortable Umgebungen entstehen können. Im Winter können die Eigentümer den nördlichen Bereich des Hauses benutzen, auf den die Sonne fällt. Von der Terrasse auf der Südseite aus hat man einen wunderschönen Blick auf den Hafen.

This flexible area made up of the living room, kitchen and dining room crosses the entire breadth of the house.

Une zone polyvalente, accueillant la salle de séjour, la cuisine et la salle à manger, aux pavés de pierre, est l'unique superficie qui traverse la largeur de la maison.

Die einzige Zone, die die Breite des Hauses kreuzt, ist ein kombinierter Bereich mit Wohnzimmer, Küche und dem mit Steinen gepflasterten Speisezimmer.

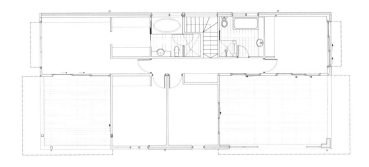

› Second floor   Deuxième étage   Zweites Obergeschoss

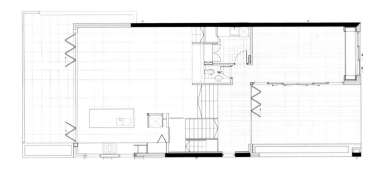

› First floor   Premier étage   Erstes Obergeschoss

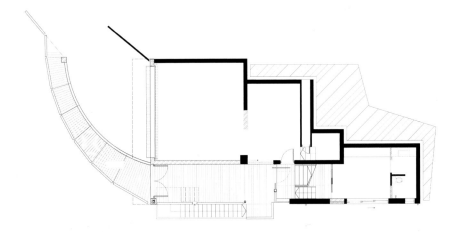

› Ground floor   Rez-de-chaussée   Erdgeschoss

Råman Residence

Maison Råman

Haus Råman

This country house, formerly a typical Swedish rural school, features natural stone façades painted white, giving an even, straightforward appearance. The house is set on various levels, so that the meticulously planned inner space can benefit from an original lighting scheme. The old classrooms were converted into a spacious kitchen, a dining room and large study. The main bedroom and guest bedroom were assigned to the upper floor. The seating, the matching furniture, and the white-painted pine floors all help create an original style; furthermore, the fitted wardrobes and centrally-placed bed emphasize the generous dimensions of the sleeping quarters. A hall separating the two bedrooms is lit by an artificial light placed near the floor.

Cette maison de campagne, ancienne école rurale suédoise, présente des façades de pierre naturelle peintes en blanc, lui conférant une apparence claire et sobre. L'habitation décline différents niveaux, permettant à l'espace intérieur, soigneusement planifié, de concevoir un éclairage original. Les anciennes salles de classe ont été redistribuées en large cuisine, en salle à manger et en studio aux dimensions généreuses. La chambre à coucher principale et celle d'amis se trouvent à l'étage supérieur. Les fauteuils et les meubles hétérogènes et les sols de pin peints en blanc créent un style original. En outre, les armoires encastrées et le lit situé au centre, exaltent les proportions généreuses de la chambre à coucher. Un vestibule séparant les chambres à coucher, est éclairé par une source de lumière artificielle située près du sol.

Dieses Haus auf dem Lande, das früher eine typische schwedische Landschule war, hat eine weiß gestrichene Fassade aus Naturstein, die es glatt und einfach wirken lässt. Das Haus unterteilt sich innen in verschiedene, sorgfältig geplante Ebenen, die dazu benutzt werden, eine originelle Beleuchtung zu schaffen. Die ehemaligen Klassenzimmer wurden in eine große Küche, ein Speisezimmer und ein großes Atelier umgebaut. Das Hauptschlafzimmer und das Gästezimmer befinden sich im Obergeschoss. Die einheitlichen Stühle und Möbel sowie der weiß gestrichene Boden aus Kiefer wirken sehr originell, und durch die Einbauschränke und das Bett mitten im Raum wird noch die Größe des Schlafzimmers unterstrichen. Die Diele zwischen den beiden Schlafzimmern wird durch ein künstliches Licht in Bodennähe beleuchtet.

The classrooms in this former rural schoolhouse are spacious and well lit.

Les salles de classe de l'ancienne école rurale génèrent des espaces à la fois généreux et lumineux.

Die Klassenräume der ehemaligen Landschule sind groß und hell.

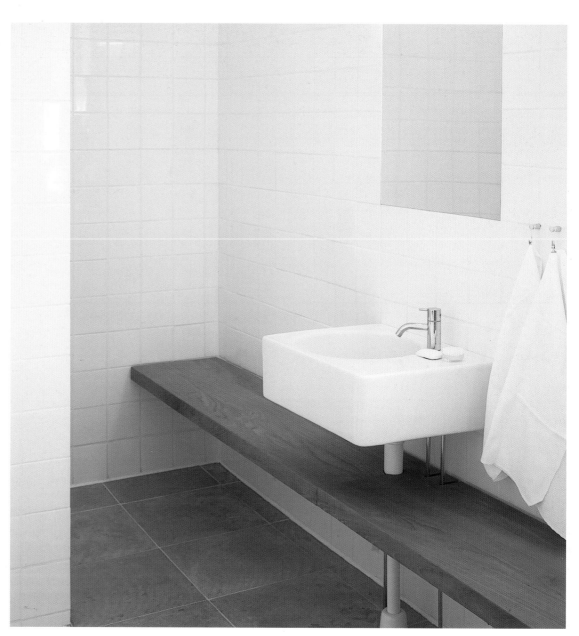

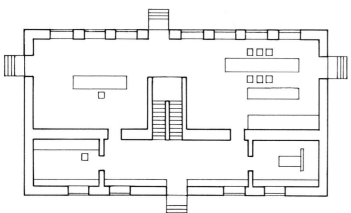

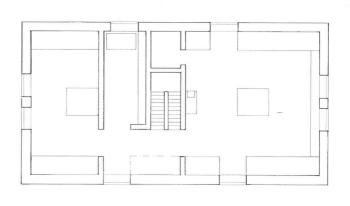

› Ground floor Rez-de-chaussée Erdgeschoss

› First floor Premier étage Erstes Obergeschoss

A long, artificially lit niche above the floor lights up the hallway between the two bedrooms.

Le vestibule, qui sépare les deux chambres à coucher, est éclairé par une source de lumière artificielle située dans une niche au-dessus du sol.

Eine Diele zwischen den beiden Schlafzimmern wird durch ein künstliches Licht in Bodennähe beleuchtet.

House in Telluride
Maison à Telluride
Haus in Telluride

Discreetly hidden in the midst of buildings typical of the region, this house—situated close to the Telluride ski resort—, presents a traditional appearance. The façaces are covered with natural stone and aged timber, creating a less elaborated effect than that of the neighboring houses. Inside, the communal areas, which include the living room, kitchen and dining room, have been located on the second floor, so as to benefit from the mountain views. The first floor houses the private areas, such as the bathroom and the bedrooms. The bathroom is directly linked to the master bedroom and the glass panels of the shower booth double as a headboard for the bed. Fluorescent tubes provide indirect light and also give a contemporary feel to the space.

Implantée discrètement dans un cadre de constructions typiques de la zone, cette habitation, située près de la station de ski de Telluride, offre une structure traditionnelle dotée d'une toiture à deux pentes. Les façades sont recouvertes de bois vieilli et de pierre naturelle, conférant à l'ensemble une impression plus pure et simple que celle des autres maisons environnantes. A l'intérieur, les zones communes, à savoir, la salle de séjour, la cuisine et la salle à manger, se situent au deuxième étage pour profiter des vues sur la montagne. Le premier étage accueille les zones privées comme la salle de bains, la chambre à coucher et les chambres individuelles. La salle de bains est directement reliée à la chambre à coucher où les panneaux de verre de la douche servent de tête de lit. Les tubes fluorescents créent un éclairage indirect, conférant à l'espace un aspect contemporain.

Dieses Haus, das sich diskret zwischen die typischen Bauten der Region einfügt, befindet sich in der Nähe der Skistation Telluride. Es besitzt eine traditionelle Struktur mit einem Satteldach. Die Fassaden sind mit Naturstein und gealtert wirkendem Holz verkleidet, so dass es einfacher aussieht als die Häuser der Umgebung. Die gemeinsamen Räume wie das Wohnzimmer, die Küche und das Speisezimmer befinden sich im zweiten Stock, von dem aus man einen schönen Blick auf die Berge hat. In der ersten Etage liegen die privaten Räume wie das Bad, das Schlafzimmer und die Zimmer der Familienmitglieder. Das Bad ist direkt mit dem Schlafzimmer verbunden und die Glastüren der Dusche sind gleichzeitig das Kopfteil des Bettes. Durch Leuchtstoffröhren wurde eine indirekte Beleuchtung geschaffen, die die Wohnumgebung sehr zeitgenössisch wirken lässt.

In this minimalist space, a fireplace of contemporary design serves both functional and decorative purposes.

Dans cet espace minimaliste, la cheminée au design contemporain est, en même temps, un élément fonctionnel et décoratif.

In diesem minimalistischen Raum ist der moderne Kamin gleichzeitig ein funktionelles und ein dekoratives Element.

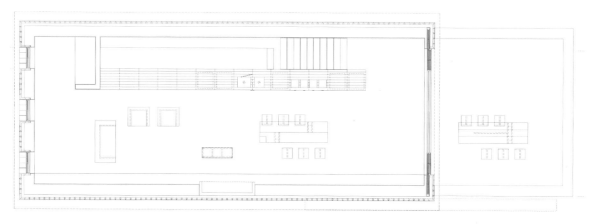

› **Plan** Plan Grundriss

The glass panels enclosing the shower booth double as a headboard for the bed. The choice of materials reflects the architect's personal style.

Les panneaux de verre de la douche font aussi office de tête de lit. Le choix des matériaux reflète le style particulier de l'architecte.

Die Glasplatten der Duschkabine lassen sich zusammenklappen und als Kopfbrett des Bettes benutzen. Die Wahl der Materialen spiegelt den persönlichen Stil des Architekten wider.

Holiday Retreat
Refuge de vacances
Zufluchtsort für die Ferien

In this residence, which occupies a 6,600-sq.-ft plot, the architects created horizontal and vertical spaces that serve various functions. The design avoided levelling the land and instead successfully faced the challenges of placement: situated next to an alpine meadow, converted into a ski run in winter, the house was raised to capture the sun's rays and enjoy the spectacular views. At the same time, a dialog is established with the environment, as the surrounding meadow remains untouched. The external appearance reinvents the typical concept of the wide, low chalet with dark wooden cladding and small windows, by transforming it into a dark wooden tower with large openings.

Dans cette résidence, occupant un terrain de 630 m², les architectes ont créé des espaces horizontaux et verticaux aux fonctions multiples. Leur design refuse de niveler le terrain dans la construction du programme et assume avec brio les difficultés liées à son implantation : située à côté d'un alpage, transformé en piste de ski l'hiver, la maison s'élève pour capter les rayons de soleil et apprivoiser les vues spectaculaires. En même temps, elle instaure un dialogue avec l'environnement, puisque autour de la maison le pré reste intact. L'extérieur réinvente le thème récurent du chalet bas et large, doté de revêtements en bois sombre et de petites fenêtres, pour le transformer en une tour de bois sombre aux grandes ouvertures.

In diesem Haus, das ein Grundstück von 630 m² einnimmt, schufen die Architekten waagerechte und senkrechte Räume, die vielen verschiedenen Funktionen dienen. Dabei wollte man es vermeiden, das Grundstück zu begradigen, um alle notwendigen Räume schaffen zu können, und die Architekten planten mit großem Erfolg eine Wohnumgebung, die dem schwierigen Standort gerecht wird. Das Haus liegt auf einer Wiese in den Alpen, die im Winter zur Skipiste wird, und es ragt nach oben, so dass die Sonnenstrahlen einfallen und man einen wundervollen Blick hat. Gleichzeitig entsteht ein Dialog mit der Umgebung, weil die Wiese, die das Haus umgibt, unangetastet blieb. Von außen wirkt das Haus wie eine neue Interpretation eines niedrigen und breiten Hauses, das mit dunklem Holz verkleidet ist, kleine Fenster hat und in einen dunklen Turm aus Holz mit großen Öffnungen verwandelt wurde.

This project envisaged the absence of traditional rooms, as these are replaced by vertical and horizontal spaces serving different purposes.

Le projet se base sur le concept d'une ambiance unique : il n'y a pas de pièces, mais des espaces verticaux et horizontaux qui revêtent diverses fonctions.

Es sollte ein einziger Raum entstehen, es gibt keine Zimmer, sondern waagerechte und senkrechte Bereiche, die verschiedenen Funktionen dienen.

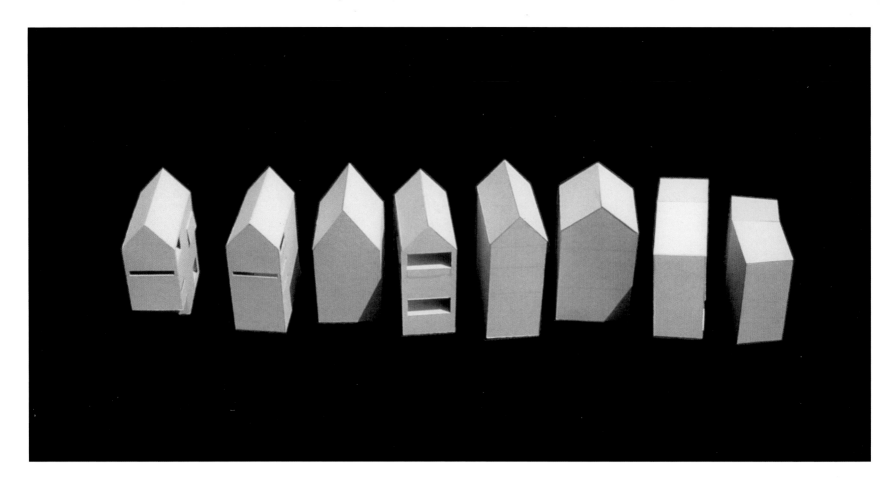

› Plans Plans Grundrisse

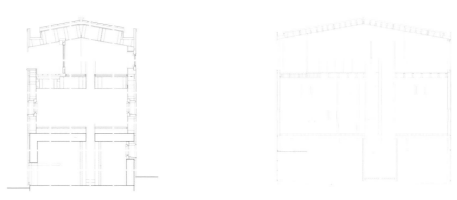

› Sections Sections Schnitte

Two-family Duplex
Duplex pour deux familles
Zweifamilienhaus

The layout for this maisonette construction on the outskirts of Basel demonstrates the close interaction that can be achieved through location and structure, showing how a large space can be subtly integrated into the landscape. Two homes of a similar size, set on a concrete base, climb the slope to the hilltop, hugging the terrain. The two stairways on the northern facade cross each other, uniting upstairs and downstairs sections and, at the same time, neatly reducing circulation space by doubling as a corridor. The large sliding windows between this level and the prefabricated structure are protected by a sunscreen of wooden slats. When closed, the windows appear to have no frames; when open, however, they simply disappear from view. Reducing the windows to mere openings establishes a direct link between the environment outside and the interior of the house.

Le plan de ce duplex situé dans les faubourgs de Bâle, est l'exemple de l'étroite interaction qui peut se créer entre l'emplacement et la structure, et montre qu'un grand espace peut s'intégrer subtilement au paysage. Les habitations de même taille reposent sur un socle de béton permettant à la structure de vaincre la pente et d'atteindre la colline. Les deux escaliers croisés, adjacents à la face nord de l'édifice, unissent les deux niveaux des habitations et servent de couloirs, réduisant avec élégance la zone de passage. Les liteaux de bois servent également d'écran aux grandes fenêtres coulissantes, disposées entre ce niveau et la structure préfabriquée. Fermées, les fenêtres semblent fixes et dépourvues de cadre, ouvertes, elles disparaissent tout simplement. La réduction des fenêtres à de simples ouvertures est l'expression du lien direct entre le milieu existant et l'univers intérieur de la maison.

Der Grundriss dieser zweistöckigen Wohnung am Stadtrand von Basel ist ein gutes Beispiel für die enge Verbindung, die zwischen dem Standort und der Struktur entstehen kann. Hier wird bewiesen, wie sich ein großes Haus subtil in die Landschaft einfügen kann. Die gleich großen Wohnungen haben eine Basis aus Beton, die es möglich macht, dass sich die Struktur am Hang entlang bis zum Hügel erstreckt. Die beiden gekreuzten Treppen, die an der Nordseite des Hauses liegen, vereinen die beiden Etagen der Wohnungen und dienen als Flur, wobei sie auf elegante Weise den Durchgangsbereich minimalisieren. Holzlatten schützen die großen Schiebefenster, die sich zwischen dieser Etage und der vorgefertigten Struktur befinden. Wenn die Fenster geschlossen sind, wirken sie fest und rahmenlos, wenn sie geöffnet sind, verschwinden sie einfach. Die Reduktion der Fenster zu einfachen Öffnungen drückt die Idee aus, eine direkte Verbindung zwischen der existierenden Umgebung und der inneren Welt des Hauses zu schaffen.

The natural environment inspired the architect to design this home, fully integrated with its surroundings through the use of natural materials.

Le paysage champêtre des environs a inspiré l'architecte dans la construction d'une habitation qui s'intègre parfaitement à l'environnement grâce à ses matériaux naturels.

Die karge Landschaft inspirierte die Architekten bei der Planung dieses Hauses, das sich aufgrund der Naturmaterialien und einfachen Formen perfekt in die Umgebung einfügt.

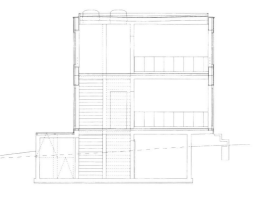
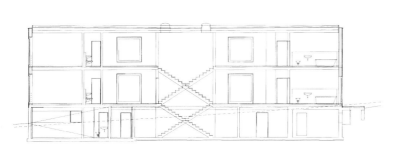

› Sections Sections Schnitte

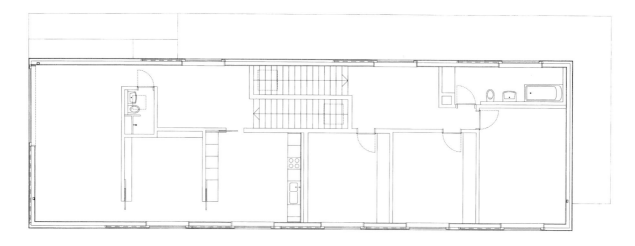

› Second floor   Deuxième étage   Zweites Obergeschoss

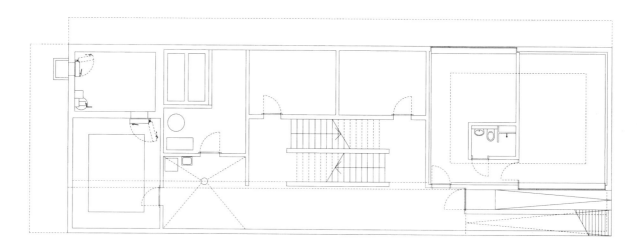

› First floor   Premier étage   Erstes Obergeschoss

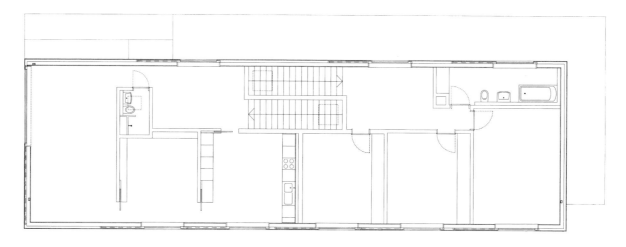

› Ground floor   Rez-de-chaussée   Erdgeschoss

Wonderful views of the forest are enjoyed from every room in the house.

Toutes les pièces de la maison, bénéficient de merveilleuses vues sur la forêt.

Von allen Zimmern des Hauses aus hat man einen wundervollen Blick auf den Wald.

Tucson Mountain Residence

Maison de montagne à Tucson

Berghaus in Tucson

This house, situated in a vast desert landscape with cacti and shrubs, merges into the environment as a result of a careful selection of materials and shapes, giving rise to a structure that integrates perfectly into the dramatic scenery. The crinkly structure of the roof blends with the earthy colors of the surrounding environment, in an attempt to harmonise architecture with nature. The mixture of mud and cement used in the construction provides a high degree of waterproofing, interior acoustic insulation and fire proofing. The interior design concept is simple and minimalist, combining aesthetics with functionality. The high roofs reflect the heat, whilst the materials conserve heat during the night, which is often cold.

Cette habitation, implantée dans un vaste paysage désertique où poussent les cactus et les arbustes se fond au paysage grâce à une sélection bien étudiée de matériaux et formes, donnant lieu à une structure complètement intégrée au paysage grandiose. La structure plissée de la couverture se confond avec les tons terreux des alentours, dans un souci d'harmonie entre architecture et paysage. Le mélange de boue et de ciment utilisé dans la construction lui confère une grande imperméabilité, isole l'intérieur contre les bruits et le feu. Le concept qui régit le design intérieur est simple et minimaliste, combinant esthétique et fonctionnalisme. Les hauts plafonds diffusent la chaleur, tandis que les matériaux utilisés la conservent la nuit, où il fait en généralement plus froid.

Dieses Haus liegt inmitten einer Wüstenlandschaft, in der Kakteen und Sträucher wachsen. Die Materialien und Formen wurden so gewählt, dass der Bau praktisch in der Landschaft verschwindet und sich seine Struktur völlig in diese kraftvolle Umgebung einpasst. Die faltige Dachstruktur vermischt sich mit den Erdtönen der Umgebung, so dass eine große Harmonie zwischen der Architektur und der Landschaft entstand. Die Mischung aus Ton und Zement, die für den Bau benutzt wurde, macht das Haus sehr wasserfest, sorgt für Geräuschdämpfung und dient als Schutz vor Feuer. Das Konzept der Innengestaltung ist einfach und minimalistisch: Ästhetik wird mit Funktionalität kombiniert. Die hohen Decken verteilen die Hitze, während die verwendeten Baustoffe in den kalten Nächten die Wärme speichern.

The crinkly structure of the roof blends with the earthy tones of the surrounding environment, in an attempt to harmonise architecture with nature.

Dans un souci d'harmonie entre architecture et paysage, la structure plissée de la couverture se confond avec les tons terreux des alentours.

Die faltige Dachstruktur vermischt sich mit den Erdtönen der Umgebung, so dass eine große Harmonie zwischen der Architektur und der Landschaft entstand.

The mixture of mud and cement employed in the construction gives a high degree of waterproofing, interior acoustic insulation and protection against fire.

Le mélange de boue et de ciment utilisé dans la construction lui octroie une grande imperméabilité, tout en isolant l'intérieur contre les bruits et le feu.

Die Mischung aus Ton und Zement, die für die Struktur benutzt wurde, macht das Haus sehr wasserfest, sorgt für Geräuschdämpfung und dient als Schutz vor Feuer.

High ceilings disperse heat, whilst the materials used retain it through the cold nights.

Les hauts plafonds diffusent la chaleur et les matériaux utilisés la conservent la nuit, où il fait en généralement plus froid.

Die hohen Decken verteilen die Hitze, während die benutzten Materialien in den kalten Nächten die Wärme speichern.

Willimann-Lötscher Residence

Maison Willimann-Lötscher

Haus Willimann-Lötscher

This house is situated between a hillside slope and the end of another range of hills, on the outskirts of the town of Sevgein, with a view of the Upper Rhine valley. The houses wooden structure was prefabricated in sections: on both facades and the roof, the standard windows for pitched roof dwellings were used. The clients, a family of four, wanted a house with many rooms, like a kind of maze. The result is a tower-like construction tailored to the sloping ground, with a central staircase that acts as a vertebral column. Each floor has two rooms, arranged along the wall to create a vertical spiral inside the house—a sort of internal topography—and thereby maximize the inner space, notwithstanding the reduced size of the individual rooms.

Cette habitation est située entre un coteau et le bout d'une série de collines, dans les environs du village de Sevgein, emplacement permettant de contempler la vallée du Haut-Rhin. L'ossature de bois de la maison est constituée de panneaux préfabriqués. Les deux façades et la toiture accueillent des fenêtres, employées d'habitude dans les toitures à deux pentes. Le client, une famille de quatre personnes, voulait une maison avec un grand nombre de chambres, une espèce de labyrinthe. Il en résulte une construction en forme de tour qui s'adapte à l'inclinaison du terrain, avec un escalier central qui en est la colonne vertébrale. Chaque étage héberge deux chambres situées le long du même mur afin de créer une spirale verticale à l'intérieur de la maison -une espèce de topographie interne- et de maximiser le volume intérieur, malgré les dimensions réduites des chambres.

Dieses Haus liegt an einem Hang am Ende einer Hügelkette am Stadtrand von Sevgein, von wo aus man einen Blick auf das Oberrheintal hat. Die Holzstruktur des Hauses wurde in Sektionen vorgefertigt. An beiden Fassaden und im Dach wurden Fenster eingesetzt, wie sie normalerweise bei Satteldächern verwendet werden. Die Kunden, eine vierköpfige Familie, wollten ein Haus mit vielen Zimmern, so eine Art Labyrinth. So entstand ein Haus, das wie ein Turm aussieht und sich an die Neigung des Geländes anschmiegt. In diesem Haus befindet sich eine zentrale Treppe, die eine Art Wirbelsäule bildet. In jeder Etage liegen an der gleichen Wand zwei Zimmer, so dass eine Art vertikale Spirale im Haus entstand, eine Art innere Geländeform. Obwohl die Zimmer sehr klein sind, wurde der vorhandene Raum optimal ausgenutzt.

This house is situated between a hillside slope and the end of another range of hills, on the outskirts of the town of Sevgein, with a view of the Upper Rhine valley.

La maison est située entre un coteau et le bout d'une série de collines, dans les environs du village de Sevgein, emplacement qui lui permet de contempler la vallée du Haut-Rhin.

Dieses Haus liegt an einem Hang am Ende einer Reihe von Hügeln, am Stadtrand von Sevgein, von wo aus man einen Blick auf das Oberrheintal hat.

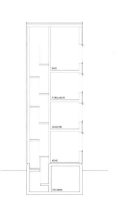

› **Sections** Sections Schnitte

› **Location plan** Plan de situation Umgebungsplan

House No. 19
Maison N.º 19
Haus Nr. 19

This house is extremely simple: the raw and plain building materials determine the quality of the space. The internal lighting is especially bright and beautiful, and the large windows allow the interior to relate directly and powerfully with the exterior. This mobile studio is part of the Utrecht community art project. The basic idea is a long space that can be divided into various areas, both internally and externally. The construction is very simple: the walls, floor and roof are made entirely of wooden panelling joined together with steel ties. In spite of its mobility, it is a large, robust and permanent construction, sufficiently sturdy to be transported in one piece.

Cette maison est d'une extrême simplicité : le matériau de construction, rugueux et brut, définit la qualité de l'espace. La lumière intérieure est particulièrement vive et belle, et grâce aux grandes baies, la relation entre l'extérieur et l'intérieur est directe et puissante. Ce studio mobil fait partie d'un programme d'art communal d'Utrecht. Le projet consiste en un espace allongé pouvant être divisé en diverses zones intérieures et extérieures. Sa construction est très simple : les murs, le sol et la toiture sont entièrement fabriqués en panneaux de bois joints par des charnières d'acier. Malgré sa mobilité, c'est un grand espace, robuste et solide, suffisamment stable pour être transporté en un seul bloc.

Es handelt sich um ein extrem einfaches Haus, bei dem das rohe und grobe Baumaterial das Aussehen der Räumlichkeiten bestimmt. Durch die großen Fensterläden fällt ein besonders schönes und lebendiges Licht ein, und die Verbindung zwischen innen und außen ist sehr direkt und kraftvoll. Dieses mobile Atelier bildet einen Teil des städtischen Kunstprogramms von Utrecht. Es sollte ein länglicher Raum geschaffen werden, der in verschiedene Innen- und Außenbereiche aufgeteilt werden kann. Die Bauweise ist sehr einfach, die Wände, der Boden und das Dach bestehen aus Holzpaneelen, die mit Stahlverbindungen befestigt sind. Trotz ihrer Beweglichkeit ist die dauerhafte Konstruktion groß und robust genung, um in einem Stück transportiert zu werden.

In spite of its mobility, it is a large, robust and permanent construction, sufficiently sturdy to be transported in one piece.

Malgré sa flexibilité, la maison est grande, robuste et solide, et suffisamment stable pour être transportée d'une seule pièce.

Trotz ihrer Beweglichkeit ist die dauerhafte Konstruktion groß und robust genung, um in einem Stück transportiert zu werden.

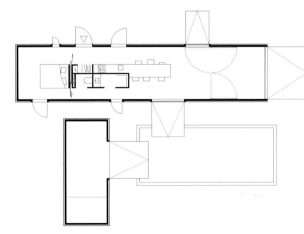
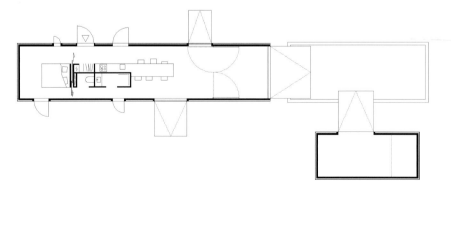

› Plans Plans Grundrisse

130

House in Bergen

Maison à Bergen

Haus in Bergen

This house, designed by Marc Prosman's team of architects, has a U-shape floor plan open to the wood at the rear. Since the site is above street level, a garage was built beneath the ground floor, where all the domestic functions are congregated. The roof on the annex behind one of the wings is designed to allow another story to be added, if necessary. The main entrance is reached across a metal catwalk, creating an unusual effect by highlighting this element linking the two volumes. The fully glazed facade provides uninterrupted views of the patio and the trees beyond. The south-facing daytime areas (dining room, kitchen and living room) may be separated by wooden sliding doors but are perceived as one large, single space.

Le design de cette maison, oeuvre de l'équipe dirigée par Marc Prosman, suit un plan en U dont le côté ouvert est orienté vers la partie arrière du terrain et un bosquet. La parcelle étant au-dessus du niveau de la rue, le garage a été installé sous le niveau principal qui accueille toutes les fonctions domestiques. Derrière une des ailes du plan en U, s'élève une annexe, dotée d'une toiture dont la pente permet de construire un niveau supplémentaire. L'accès à la maison s'effectue grâce à une passerelle métallique qui permet de visualiser l'harmonie de la structure d'entrée dans son expression particulière, unissant les deux ailes de l'édifice et dont la façade entièrement en verre permet de jouir de magnifiques vues sur le patio et la zone boisée. Les pièces diurnes (salle à manger, cuisine et salon), situées dans la zone orientée sud, sont séparées par des portes de bois coulissantes qui permettent une certaine intimité tout en donnant l'impression de se trouver dans un grand espace unique.

Dieses Haus wurde von einem Team unter der Leitung von Marc Prosman entworfen. Es hat eine U-Form und zu der zum Wald gelegenen Hinterseite geöffnet. Da die Parzelle oberhalb der Straße liegt, wurde unter der ersten Etage, die allen Wohnfunktionen dient, eine Garage angelegt. Hinter einem der Flügel des U's schuf man einen Anbau mit einem geneigten Dach, durch dessen Neigung noch eine zusätzliche Ebene eingezogen werden konnte. Den Zugang zu dem Haus bildet ein Laufsteg aus Metall, der wie ein verbindendes Element für die außergewöhnliche Struktur des Eingangs wirkt und gleichzeitig die beiden Flügel des Gebäudes miteinander verbindet. Die Fassade ist vollständig verglast, so dass man einen schönen Blick auf den Hof und den Wald hat. Die tagsüber genutzen Räume (Speisezimmer, Küche und Wohnzimmer) liegen auf der Südseite und sind durch Schiebetüren aus Holz voneinander getrennt, die für Privatsphäre sorgen, aber auch einen einzigen, großen Raum entstehen lassen können.

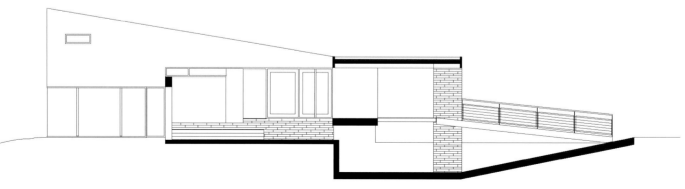

› Section Section Schnitt

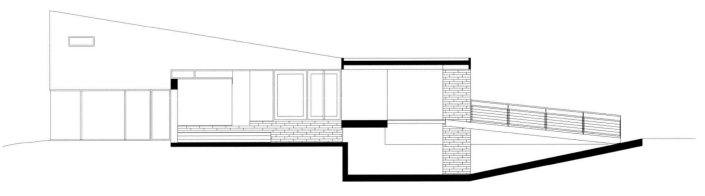

› Section Section Schnitt

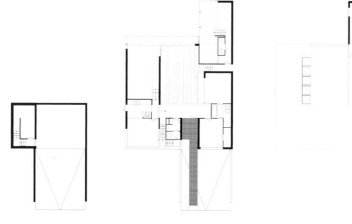

› Plans Plans Grundrisse

Minimal House
Maison minime
Minimales Haus

In designing this house, one of the main aims was to create a very small, functional and economical living space. Care was taken to ensure that this house would also harmonize fully with its lush surroundings. The chief inspiration for the designers was the setting itself, so that the house became, according to the architects themselves, a natural consequence of the landscape. Inside, a wooden passageway with a number of terraces leads to the garden. The terraces are perfectly placed to make full use of natural sunlight and provide spectacular views of the landscape, as well as a great sense of spaciousness. With this approach, furthermore, the garden counterbalances the reduced space within. Formerly a family residence, has been transformed into an architectural studio.

Un des objectifs du design de cette habitation est de créer un petit espace habitable, qui soit fonctionnel et économique. La maison, située au coeur d'une zone de végétation très dense, a été spécialement conçue pour être en harmonie avec l'environnement. Le concept essentiel qui anime le projet est ancré dans la situation même, de sorte que la maison est devenue, selon les propres termes des architectes, une réponse logique à son emplacement. A l'intérieur, un tunnel de bois aux différentes terrasses mène au jardin. La parfaite orientation des terrasses permet de profiter totalement de la lumière naturelle tout en offrant des vues spectaculaires sur l'environnement et une impression d'espace. Dans cette optique, le jardin devient également un élément qui compense la réduction de l'espace intérieur. Appartenant autrefois à une famille, est devenue par la suite un studio d'architecture.

Eines der Ziele bei dem Bau dieses Hauses war es, einen kleinen Wohnraum zu schaffen, der gleichzeitig funktionell und energiesparend ist. Das Haus befindet sich mitten in einem Gebiet mit dichter Vegetation und deshalb wurde es so entworfen, dass es sich mit dieser Umgebung im Einklang befindet. Als wichtigste Referenz für die Gestaltung des Hauses wurde der Standort genommen, so dass das Haus, wie die Architekten selbst sagen, eine logische Antwort auf den Standort ist. Im Inneren führt ein Holztunnel mit verschiedenen Terrassen in den Garten. Durch die perfekte Ausrichtung der Terrassen wird das Tageslicht maximal ausgenutzt und gleichzeitig hat man einen wundervollen Blick auf die Umgebung. Es entsteht der Eindruck von Weite. So wurde auch der Garten zu einem Element, das den knapp bemessenen Platz im Inneren ausgleicht. Das Haus, das vorher einer Familie gehörte, wurde später als Architekturstudio genutzt.

The wooden floors and walls, and the direct access to the garden, endow this house with a natural rural atmosphere.

Les sols et murs de bois, combinés à l'accès direct au jardin, créent une ambiance extrêmement naturelle et rurale.

Die Böden und Wände aus Holz und der Zugang zum Garten lassen eine natürliche und ländliche Atmosphäre entstehen.

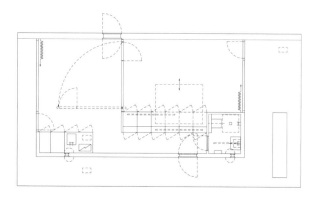

› Plan Plan Grundriss

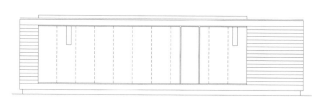

› Elevation Élévation Aufriss

Residence in Andelsbuch

Masion à Andelsbuch

Haus in Andelsbuch

This house comprises two independent homes, one on the lower floor and the other on the first floor. Each of the dwellings has two or three rooms, plus a dining room, kitchen and bathroom. It was assembled from 16x16-ft wooden units, arranged in a line and clad with prefabricated external elements. This made it possible to complete the construction in a short space of time, with minimal disruption to the environment. This was the pilot study for a series of modular buildings based on construction kits that can be adapted flexibly to suit their owners' wishes. Each house can adopt a completely different size, roof and external appearance. The modules can be combined at will, thereby building up the outline of a house. Finally, the outer coverings can be chosen from a range of ten different façade styles.

Cette maison est composée de deux habitations indépendantes, l'une située au rez-de-chaussée et l'autre au premier étage. Chaque habitation comprend deux ou trois chambres, un salon/salle à manger, une cuisine et une salle de bains. Sa construction a été faite à base de modules de bois de 5x5 m, disposés en ligne et revêtus d'éléments de façade préfabriqués. Cette modalité de construction permet de réaliser la maison en très peu de temps avec un impact minime sur l'environnement. C'est un projet pilote d'une série d'édifices modulaires basés sur le principe des jeux de construction, modulables au gré des désirs des propriétaires. Chaque maison peut revêtir une forme, un gabarit, un toit et un aspect extérieur totalement différent. Les modules peuvent être combinés à volonté, pour créer la silhouette de la maison. En fin de compte, il est possible de choisir l'enveloppe extérieure parmi dix types de façade différents.

In diesem Haus befinden sich zwei unabhängige Wohnungen, eine im Erdgeschoss und eine in der ersten Etage. Jede der Wohnungen verfügt über zwei oder drei Zimmer, ein kombiniertes Wohn- und Speisezimmer, eine Küche und ein Bad. Als Konstruktionsmaterial dienten 5x5 m große Holzmodule, die in einer Linie angeordnet und mit vorgefertigten Fassadenelementen verkleidet wurden. So konnte man in kürzester Zeit ein Haus errichten, das die natürliche Umgebung nur geringfügig beschädigt hat. Es handelt sich hier um das erste Modell einer Reihe von modularen Gebäuden, die auf Grundlage eines Spiels mit den Konstruktionen errichtet wurden, und die man ganz flexibel an die Ansprüche der Eigentümer anpassen kann. Jedes Haus kann eine eigene Form und Größe haben. Die Module können nach Belieben kombiniert werden, so dass jedes Mal ein anderes Haus entsteht. Auch bei der Außenverkleidung kann unter zehn verschiedenen Fassadentypen ausgewählt werden.

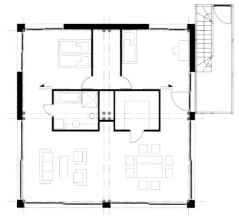

› Plan Plan Grundriss

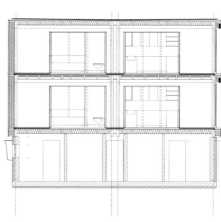

› Section Section Schnitt

Levin Residence
Résidence Levin
Haus Levin

The design goals of this house, apart from accomodating a family with three children, were to take full advantage of the view of the bay and create a space that could contain approximately 300 people. A spiral staircase that gives access to the different levels provides the focal point in a stark, light and flexible composition. The rectangular layout, which is the basis of the program, contrasts with the curved forms, wich respond to various needs. A minimalist idiom and the extensive use of glass gives priority to the views. A series of sliding panels and screens achieve the required degree of flexibility, integrating or dividing the spaces from each other, or from the exterior.

L'objectif du design de cette maison était, au-delà d'accueillir une famille ses trois enfants, d'exploiter au maximum la vue sur la baie et d'obtenir un espace que puisse héberger environ 300 personnes. Une composition pure, légère et flexible part du point de mire de la maison, un escalier en colimaçon, desservant les différents niveaux. Le schéma rectangulaire, qui est la base du programme, contraste avec les formes incurvées, répondant aux diverses fonctions. Un langage minimaliste et l'emploi du verre dans tous les espaces élèvent les vues au rang de protagoniste. Une série de panneaux coulissants et de paravents créent l'univers modulable recherché, intégrant ou divisant les espaces entre eux ou avec l'extérieur.

Das Ziel bei der Planung dieses Hauses war es, ein Heim für eine Familie mit drei Kindern zu bauen, den Blick auf die Bucht so weit wie möglich freizugeben und einen Raum zu schaffen, in dem ungefähr 300 Personen Platz haben. Ausgehend von einem Mittelpunkt in Form einer Wendeltreppe, die auf die verschiedenen Ebenen führt, wurde eine saubere, leichte und flexible Anlage geschaffen. Das rechteckige Schema des gesamten Hauses bildet einen Gegensatz zu den kurvigen Formen, die aus verschiedenen Gründen entstanden. Der minimalistische Stil und viel Glas in allen Räumen machen aus dem Ausblick das wichtigste dekorative Element. Durch eine Reihe von verschiebbaren Paneelen und Schirmen wurde die gewünschte Beweglichkeit erreicht, so dass man die verschiedenen Räume miteinander oder mit der Umgebung verbinden oder voneinander trennen kann.

The house consists of a plain flat facade decorated with vertical panels and an arched steel roof.

La maison est constituée d'une façade lisse et simple, agrémentée de panneaux verticaux et d'une toiture en acier.

Das Haus hat eine einfache und glatte Fassade, die mit vertikalen Paneelen und einem gewellten Stahldach dekoriert ist.

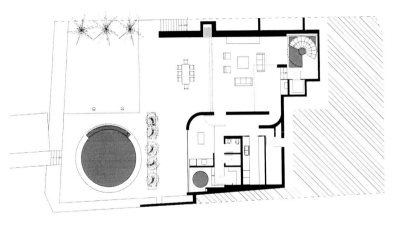

› Ground floor   Rez-de-chaussée   Erdgeschoss

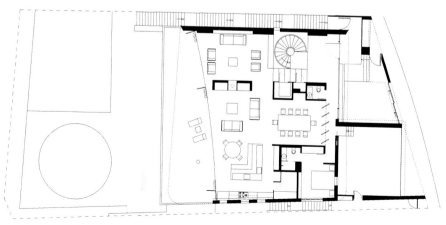

› Second floor   Deuxième étage   Zweites Obergeschoss

Glass Interface

Interface de verre

Schnittstelle aus Glas

The facade of this house is a combination of a glass screen and a green sunlight filter that acts as an interface between the building and the street outside, as well as providing diffuse lighting to the spacious interior. The rooms are finished with white walls and wooden floors, which maintain an unbroken relationship with the exterior via terraces, large windows and skylights. Dividing walls or sliding doors separate the various areas inside the house. In the main living room, the floor surface is enhanced by means of light wooden planks, interspersed at alternating right angles by white tiles, from which a spiral staircase emerges to climb up to the bedrooms.

La façade de cette maison offre un mélange entre un écran de verre et un filtre vert servant d'interface entre l'édifice et la rue, procurant une lumière diffuse dans les intérieurs spacieux. Les chambres sont composées de murs blancs et de sols en bois qui assurent, à tout moment, une relation avec l'extérieur par le biais de terrasses, de grandes baies vitrées ou de lucarnes. Cloisons et portes coulissantes séparent les différentes zones de l'habitation. Dans le salon principal, la superficie du sol ressort grâce à des lattes en bois de couleur claire, interrompues à chaque angle droit par des carreaux blancs, d'où surgit un escalier en colimaçon qui mène aux chambres.

Die Fassade dieses Hauses ist eine Kombination aus einem Glasschirm und einem grünen Filter. Sie bildet die Schnittstelle zwischen dem Gebäude und der Straße und versorgt die Räume gleichzeitig mit diffusem Licht. Die Zimmer haben weiße Wände und Holzfußböden und sind über die Terrassen, große Fenster und Dachfenster überall mit der Außenwelt verbunden. Um die verschiedenen Bereiche der Wohnung voneinander zu trennen, benutzte man Zwischenwände und Schiebetüren. Im Wohnzimmer wird der Boden durch helle Holztafeln hervorgehoben, die in geraden, aufeinanderfolgenden Winkeln durch weiße Bodenfliesen unterbrochen werden, aus denen eine Wendeltreppe heraussteigt, die zu den Schlafzimmern führt.

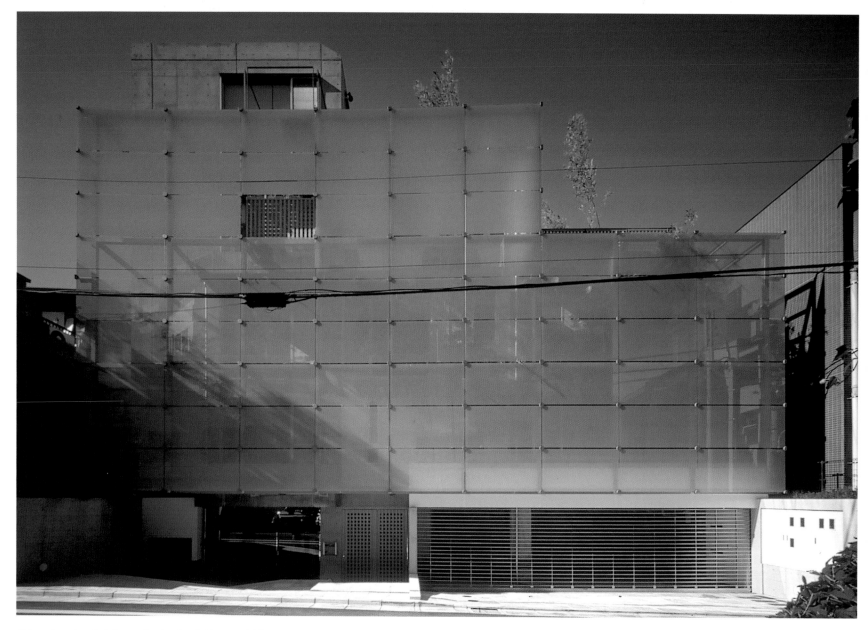

Pale-colored materials emphasize the lightness of this structure.

Les matériaux de couleurs claires rehaussent la légèreté de la structure entière.

Die Materialien in hellen Farben unterstreichen die Leichtigkeit der gesamten Struktur.

A large communal room has a glass roof supported by the beams extending from the glass doors.

Une grande habitation à usage commun est dotée d'un toit de verre reposant sur des poutres qui s'étirent le long des portes de verre.

Ein großer, gemeinsamer Raum hat eine Glasdecke, die von Säulen gestützt wird, die an den Glastüren entlang verlaufen.

On the exterior, the glass panels project sparkling reflections when the interior is filled with natural light.

Depuis l'extérieur, les panneaux de verre irradient un scintillement lumineux qui se traduit directement par l'éclairage des espaces intérieurs de lumière naturelle.

Von außen glitzern die Glasscheiben, und im Inneren durchflutet Tageslicht die Räume.

O House
Maison O
Haus O

Surrounded by hills and open countryside, this house establishes a close relationship with the landscape, through its placement, form and materials. The whole structure resembles a solid rock enveloped by a membrane determining the various views from the inside. The house has a semi-private terrace facing east. A projecting roof provides shade to the outside terrace and also to the interior spaces. Inside, the house is an expression of contemporary lifestyle. The lighting, primarily using natural sources from the windows, is complemented with light sources set in the remotest corners. The space under the stairs acts as a partition between the living room and the kitchen.

Au coeur de champs et collines, cette habitation établit une relation étroite avec la topographie par le biais de son orientation, de sa forme et de ses matériaux. La structure se présente à l'instar d'un rocher massif enveloppé d'une membrane qui oriente et structure les différentes vues depuis l'intérieur de la maison. L'habitation abrite un patio intérieur semi privé orienté Est. Une toiture en saillie procure de l'ombre à la terrasse extérieure et aux espaces intérieurs. A l'intérieur, cette maison offre une réflexion sur le mode de vie contemporain. L'éclairage, bénéficiant de la lumière naturelle qui entre par les baies vitrées, est complété par des sources de lumière dans les zones plus retirées. La cage d'escalier sert de division et sépare la zone de séjour de la cuisine.

Dieses von offenen Feldern und Hügeln umgebene Haus stellt über seine Ausrichtung, Form und die verwendeten Materialien eine enge Verbindung zum Gelände her. Die Struktur wirkt wie ein massiver Felsen, der mit einem Film bedeckt ist, der die verschiedenen Ausblicke, die man vom Inneren hat, bestimmt. Zu dem Haus gehört ein halbprivater Innenhof in Ostrichtung. Ein überstehendes Dach spendet der Außenterrasse und den Innenräumen Schatten. Im Inneren ist das Haus Ausdruck einer modernen Lebensweise. Für die Beleuchtung wurde das Tageslicht ausgenutzt, das durch die Fenster fällt. Dieses Licht wird in den weiter innen liegenden Bereichen durch andere Lichtquellen unterstützt. Ein Hohlraum unter der Treppe dient der Raumteilung, denn er trennt das Wohnzimmer von der Küche.

The house has a secluded inner patio facing east. A jutting roof provides shade to both the outdoor terrace and the inner spaces.

L'habitation abrite un patio intérieur semi privé orienté Est. Une toiture en saillie procure de l'ombre à la terrasse extérieure et aux espaces intérieurs.

Zu dem Haus gehört ein halbprivater Innenhof in Ostrichtung. Ein überstehendes Dach spendet der Außenterrasse und den Innenräumen Schatten.

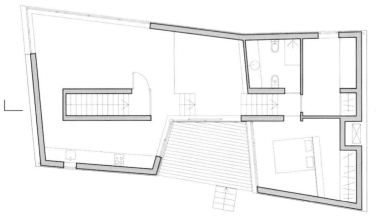

› Plan   Plan   Grundriss

› Section   Section   Schnitt

The space under the stairs acts as a partition between the living room and the kitchen.

La cage d'escalier, qui sert de cloison, sépare la zone de séjour de la cuisine.

Der Hohlraum unter der Treppe dient als Raumteiler und trennt den Wohnbereich von der Küche.

Berger House
Maison Berger
Haus Berger

To give the garden as much space as possible, the architects have placed the house perpendicular to the slope, in order to benefit from the full depth of the plot. This approach also determined the design of a recess on the ground level, which causes the second-floor level to jut out into the garden, breaking down barriers by extensive use of glass walls. This relationship between inside and out and the quest for wide-open spaces are recurrent features in this project. On the ground floor, a large interior patio is formed by means of a simple metal structure, fitted with awnings that enclose the space. Inside, the double-height dining room opens onto the garden. This solution is made possible by the fact that the only loadbearing walls present are narrow at the ends, allowing the garden to be fully enclosed in glass.

Pour obtenir un jardin spacieux, les architectes du projet ont situé la maison perpendiculaire à la pente pour bénéficier de toute la profondeur de la parcelle. Cette décision a déterminé la configuration d'un petit renfoncement au niveau inférieur, de sorte que l'étage supérieur surplombe le jardin auquel il est relié par de grands panneaux de verre qui parviennent jusqu'au sol. Cette relation entre intérieur et extérieur et le désir d'ouvrir les espaces au maximum sont des éléments récurrents de l'habitation : le rez-de-chaussée accueille un grand patio intérieur composé d'une simple structure métallique et des toiles pour clore l'espace. A l'intérieur, la double hauteur de la salle à manger sert de lien entre les deux étages et s'ouvre sur le jardin. Cette solution est viable du fait que les uniques murs porteurs sont étroits aux extrémités, ce qui permet au jardin d'être entièrement entouré de verre.

Um mehr Platz für den Garten zu schaffen, bauten die Architekten das Haus senkrecht zur Neigung, um so die gesamte Tiefe des Grundstücks auszunutzen. Aufgrund dieser Bauweise schuf man auch eine kleine Öffnung auf der unteren Ebene, so dass das Obergesschoss über den Garten ragt und durch große Glaspaneele, die bis zum Boden reichen, mit diesem verbunden ist. Diese Beziehung zwischen innen und außen ist ein konstanter Faktor, der in der gesamten Wohnung zu finden ist. Im Erdgeschoss wurde ein großer Innenhof geschaffen, für den man eine einfache Metallstruktur und Markisen benutzte, die den Raum schließen. Im Inneren wurde die doppelte Höhe des Speisezimmers dazu benutzt, die beiden Etagen miteinander zu verbinden. Der Raum öffnet sich zum Garten. Um diese Bauweise zu ermöglichen, wurden nur an den schmalen Seiten tragende Wände errichtet, so dass man den Garten vollständig mit Glas umgeben konnte.

The extreme simplicity and elegance of form are clearly visible on the main façade, dominated by the second floor—half of which is taken up by a terrace.

La simplicité et l'élégance des formes ressortent sur la façade principale, dominée par le premier étage, où la moitié de la surface est occupée par une terrasse.

Die Einfachheit und Eleganz der Formen werden besonders an der Hauptfassade deutlich, die vom Obergeschoss beherrscht wird, in dessen Zentrum sich eine Terrasse befindet.

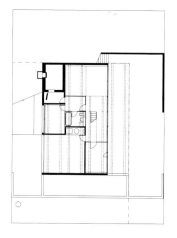

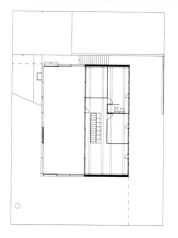

› Ground floor Rez-de-chaussée Erdgeschoss

› Basement Sous-sol Kellergeschoss

Sistek House
Maison Sistek
Haus Sistek

This house was built close to a housing estate in typical Chilean colonial style, with white façades, pastel colors and tiled roofs. Sistek House sought to break down this traditional format, plagued with monotony and repetition, to find a way to adapt the building to the hillside. The roughness of the terrain was further complicated by the size of the property, twice the usual extension in this area. The architect proposed a solution on three terraced levels, with a garden and swimming pool on the largest, bottom level; a second level devoted to everyday activities; and the sleeping quarters on the top floor of the house. This plan sought to trap a maximum of sunlight through the large windows on every façade, since the house is on the shady side of the hill. All the fully exposed areas, however, are protected by sunshades.

Cette habitation a été construite près d'une urbanisation où le style colonial chilien domine, caractérisé par les façades blanches, les couleurs pastel et les toitures de tuile. La maison Sistek voulait sortir du schéma traditionnel, monotone et répétitif, et trouver une façon de s'adapter à la colline en pente sur laquelle elle repose. A l'irrégularité du terrain, s'ajoute les dimensions de la propriété, qui occupe le double de la superficie habituelle dans cette zone. La solution proposée présente une série de trois terrasses : le niveau inférieur, le plus grand, accueille le jardin et la piscine, le niveau suivant, les zones d'activités quotidiennes et le niveau supérieur, les chambres à coucher. Cette conception tente d'exploiter au maximum la lumière solaire qui pénètre l'espace par les grandes fenêtres des façades, la maison étant située sur le côté ombragé de la colline. Par contre, les zones directement exposées au soleil sont protégées par des parasols.

Dieses Haus steht in der Nähe einer Siedlung, die vom chilenischen Kolonialstil mit seinen weißen Fassaden, Pastelltönen und Ziegeldächern geprägt ist. Das Haus Sistek schafft mit Monotonie und Wiederholungen einen Gegensatz zu dieser traditionellen Bauweise. Außerdem musste man für dieses Gebäude eine spezielle Lösung finden, um es an den Berghang anzupassen. Das Baugrundstück ist doppelt so groß wie die anderen Grundstücke in diesem Viertel. Deshalb bauten die Architekten das Haus als eine Serie von drei Terrassen. Die größte davon bildet das Untergeschoss und beherbergt den Garten und den Swimmingpool. Auf der nächsten Ebene liegen die Räume, die tagsüber genutzt werden, und ganz oben die Schlafzimmer. So wird das Sonnenlicht, das durch große Fenster in die Räume fällt, optimal ausgenutzt, was in diesem Fall sehr wichtig ist, weil das Haus auf der schattigen Seite des Hügels liegt. Alle Zonen sind durch Markisen geschützt.

The design of the façade is simple, with rectangular forms and the natural qualities contributed by the chosen materials.

La façade principale offre un design simple, résultant des formes rectangulaires et de la simplicité des matériaux utilisés.

Die Hauptfassade ist sehr einfach gestaltet. Sie ist von rechteckigen Formen und einfachen Materialien geprägt.

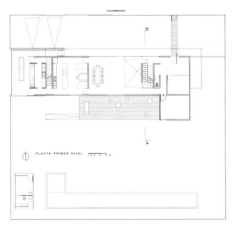

› Ground floor   Rez-de-chaussée   Erdgeschoss

› First floor   Premier étage   Erstes Obergeschoss

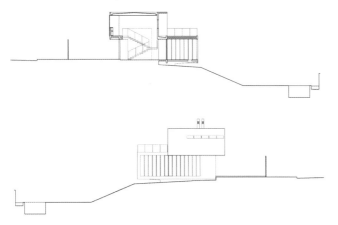

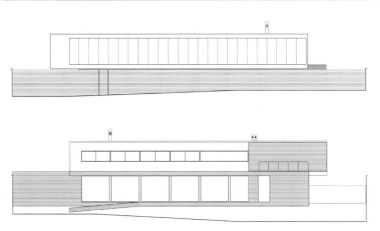

› Sections Sections Schnitte

› Elevations Élévations Aufrisse

Trickey Residence

Résidence Trickey

Haus Trickey

Situated to the east of Hawaii, this house was built on a solidified lava flow dating from 1955. The site is a protected State property. The two volumes forming the house reflect the austere forms and colours of the volcanic landscape; the polished concrete contrasts with the texture, form and color of the surrounding rocky lava. The smaller of the two volumes is transparent and contains the living area, kitchen, dining room and a guest room. The living room can be opened into a terrace by means of floor-to-ceiling sliding glass doors. The larger volume, which houses the suite, is painted a light gray, which reflects the clouds. This suite is inside a long tube closed off by glass walls and aligned in an east-west direction, parallel to the path of the sun and looking toward the volcanic crater to the west.

Située à l'est de l'archipel de Hawaï, cette maison est construite sur une coulée de lave solidifiée, datant de 1955. Le terrain est propriété de l'Etat et domaine protégé. Les deux volumes composant l'habitation reflètent les formes et les couleurs austères du paysage volcanique, et le béton poli contraste avec la texture, la forme et la couleur du paysage rocheux de lave. Le volume plus petit transparent, accueille la salle de séjour, la cuisine, la salle à manger et une chambre d'amis. La salle de séjour se transforme en terrasse grâce aux portes coulissantes en verre tout en hauteur. Le volume plus grand, qui héberge la suite, est peint d'un doux ton de gris qui reflète les nuages. Cette même suite est située à l'intérieur d'un long tube fermé de deux murs de verre, orienté est-ouest, parallèle au sens du soleil, face au cratère volcanique à l'ouest.

Dieses Haus im Osten von Hawai wurde auf einem Strom aus erstarrter Lava errichtet, der sich 1955 formte. Das Grundstück ist staatliches Eigentum und steht unter Naturschutz. Die beiden Formen, aus denen das Gebäude besteht, reflektieren die kargen Formen und Farben der Vulkanlandschaft. Polierter Beton bildet einen Gegensatz zu Textur, Form und Farbe der felsigen Lavalandschaft. Die kleinste Form des Gebäudes ist transparent. In ihr liegen das Wohnzimmer, die Küche, das Esszimmer und die Gästezimmer. Das Wohnzimmer kann mithilfe von gläsernen Schiebetüren, die vom Boden bis zur Decke reichen, in eine Terrasse verwandelt werden. In der größten Form liegt das große Schlafzimmer, das in einem zarten Grauton gestrichen ist, der die Wolken nachahmt. Dieses Schlafzimmer liegt innerhalb eines langen, durch Glaswände geschlossenen Rohrs, das von Osten nach Westen verläuft, parallel zum Verlauf der Sonne und mit Blick auf den Vulkankrater im Westen.

Polished concrete contrasts with the textures, forms and colours of the rocky lava landscape.

Le béton poli contraste avec la texture, la forme et la couleur du paysage de lave rocheuse.

Der polierte Beton bildet einen Kontrast zu der Textur, der Form und der Farbe der felsigen Lavalandschaft.

› Ground floor Rez-de-chaussée Erdgeschoss

› First floor Premier étage Erstes Obergeschoss

Residence in Greenwich

Résidence à Greenwich

Haus in Greenwich

This property is to be found in a quiet suburban neighborhood with views of the bay through the trees and nearby buildings. The brief was to create a contemporary and affordable construction that would benefit from the natural environment whilst also providing seclusion from neighbors. The rectilinear volume was placed parallel to the southern edge of the plot, and then divided into two clearly separate units: the construction on one level, facing west, acts as an entrance, whilst the main body of the house, which faces east, occupies two levels. Built from large stainless steel components, it creates a sensation of solidity, while the large openings permit a close relationship between the landscape and each of the inside spaces.

La propriété est située dans un quartier tranquille des faubourgs de la ville et jouit des vues sur la baie, perceptibles au travers des arbres et des constructions voisines. Le défi était de réaliser une construction contemporaine et rentable bénéficiant de l'environnement naturel tout en s'isolant des voisins. L'objet, aux formes rectilignes, est placé sur son axe longitudinal parallèlement à la lisière de terrain. La résidence est divisée en deux parties clairement séparées : la structure à un étage servant d'accès, orientée vers l'ouest, et le corps principal de la maison, dirigé vers l'est, sur deux niveaux. La structure, constituée de grandes pièces d'acier inoxydable, crée une impression de stabilité, tandis que les grandes ouvertures permettent une étroite relation entre le paysage et chacun des espaces.

Dieses Haus liegt in einem ruhigen Vorort und man hat einen wundervollen Blick auf die Bucht. Zwischen den Bäumen erspäht man die Nachbarhäuser. Es sollte ein zeitgenössisches und energiesparendes Haus gebaut werden, das den Bewohnern ermöglicht, die Umgebung zu genießen, aber gleichzeitig ein wenig von den Nachbarn abgeschottet zu sein. Das geradlinige Objekt liegt an einer Längsachse, die parallel zum Südrand des Grundstücks verläuft. Das Haus unterteilt sich in zwei klar voneinander getrennte Teile: eine einstöckige Struktur, die als Zugang dient und nach Westen liegt, und ein Hauptkörper, der nach Osten ausgerichtet ist und sich in zwei Ebenen unterteilt. Die Struktur besteht aus großen Edelstahlstücken und wirkt sehr solide, obwohl durch große Fenster eine enge Beziehung zwischen der Landschaft und den einzelnen Räumen geschaffen wurde.

The narrow staircase connecting both floors enjoys the natural light penetrating through the large window above, at the top of the flight of stairs.

L'étroit escalier reliant les deux étages bénéficie de la lumière qui entre par la grande fenêtre située au niveau supérieur, en haut de l'escalier.

Die enge Treppe, die die beiden Etagen miteinander verbindet, fängt das Licht auf, das durch das große Fenster im Obergeschoss am Ende der Treppe fällt.

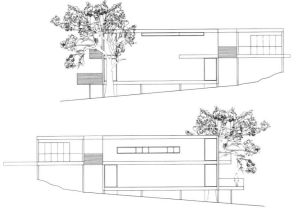

› Side elevations Elévations latérales Seitenansichten

› Front elevation Elévation frontale Frontalansicht

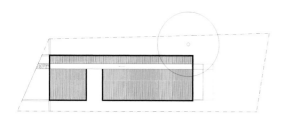

› Roof plan   Plan du toit   Dachgeschoss

› First floor   Premier étage   Erstes Obergeschoss

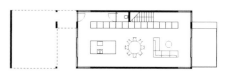

› Ground floor   Rez-de-chaussée   Erdgeschoss

Crowley Residence

Résidence Crowley

Haus Crowley

An arid landscape of undulating sand dunes, shrubs and distant mountain ranges serrating the horizon surrounds this 76-sq.-ft. property situated in southwest Texas. The exposure of the house to heat and bright light inspired a design based on the conception of frontiers and boundaries, providing an impressive panorama of the desert. The building materials, chosen to resist the region's strong winds, consist of textured concrete, stucco, galvanized steel and timber. An elongated design unifies the interior and exterior spaces, the gardens and terraces, creating shady areas, whilst the exterior spaciousness bestows a feeling of intimacy and snugness on the inner patio. The interior decor avoids unessential objects and takes full advantage of the views offered through the large windows.

Un paysage aride de dunes ondulées, d'arbustes et de lointaines montagnes ciselant l'horizon, enveloppe cette résidence de 740 m² située au sud-est du Texas. L'exposition de l'habitation à la lumière et à la chaleur, a influencé le design basé sur la création de frontières et de limites, offrant une immense vue panoramique sur le désert. Les matériaux de construction, choisis pour résister aux vents violents de la région, déclinent béton structuré, stuc, acier galvanisé et bois de Ipé. Un design allongé unit les espaces intérieurs et extérieurs, les patios et les jardins, créant des zones d'ombre. En outre, l'amplitude de l'espace extérieur convertit le patio intérieur en un lieu intime et retiré. A l'intérieur, le décor des pièces fait abstraction d'objets superflus profitant du paysage encadré, à l'instar d'un tableau, par les grandes fenêtres.

Eine karge Landschaft voller gewellter Dünen, Gestrüpp und weit entfernt liegenden Bergzügen, die sich am Horizont abzeichnen, umgibt dieses 740 m² große Haus im Südwesten Texas. Da das Haus stark dem Licht und der Hitze ausgesetzt ist, schufen die Architekten eine Reihe von Begrenzungen, durch die man auch einen überwältigenden Blick auf die umliegende Wüstenlandschaft hat. Die Baumaterialien wurden so gewählt, dass sie den starken Winden der Region widerstehen. Es handelt sich vor allem um stunkturierten Beton, Putz, verzinkten Stahl und IP-Holz. Die Innen- und Außenräume, die Höfe und die Gärten sind länglich. Es wurden Zonen mit Schatten geschaffen, und im Gegensatz zu den weiten Außenanlagen wirkt der Innenhof geschützt und heimelig. Bei der Innendekoration wurde auf alle überflüssigen Objekte verzichtet und die Landschaft selbst, umrahmt von den großen Fenstern, dient zur Dekoration.

The wooden structure above the terrace creates shady areas during the hot hours of the afternoon.

La structure de bois située sur la terrasse crée des zones d'ombre durant les heures chaudes de l'après-midi.

Die Holzstruktur über der Terrasse lässt schattige Zonen für die heißen Mittagsstunden entstehen.

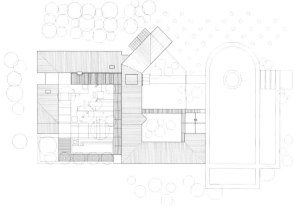

› Plan Plan Grundriss

Slope House
Maison Slope
Slope Haus

The challenge in this project was to build a home and office within a protected area, causing the minimum of environmental impact, whilst at the same time obtaining the greatest benefit from the location. Taking advantage of the natural slope of the ground, the project consists of an underground structure with few exterior surfaces, thus retaining heat to the maximum. The roof is an extension of the ground, thereby almost completely camouflaging the building whilst providing thermal insulation. Inside, the bedrooms are situated below ground level and illuminated by sloping conduits that capture daylight from various angles. All the finishing is of wood. The central part of the house is very flexible, allowing the living rooms and bedrooms to be allocated according to the owners' requirements. In order to optimize internal storage space, closets have been fitted into the dividing and side walls.

Le défi de ce projet est de construire une habitation et un bureau dans une zone protégée créant un impact minimum sur le milieu ambiant tout en tirant le meilleur parti de l'environnement. Le projet, profitant de la pente naturelle du terrain, propose une structure souterraine avec peu de surfaces extérieures, retenant un maximum de chaleur. La toiture est dans le prolongement du terrain qui camoufle presque complètement l'édifice, lui procurant une isolation thermique quasi totale. A l'intérieur, les chambres à coucher sont situées sous le niveau du sol et sont illuminées par des conduites inclinées capturant la lumière naturelle sous différents angles. Toutes les finitions sont réalisées en bois. La zone centrale de l'habitation étant très modulable, les salons et les chambres à coucher peuvent être distribués au gré des besoins des propriétaires. Pour optimiser l'espace de rangement, les armoires sont encastrées dans les cloisons et les murs latéraux.

Dieses Haus stellte eine Herausforderung an die Architekten dar, weil man eine Wohnung und ein Büro in einem geschützten Gebiet bauen musste, und die Umwelt dabei so wenig wie möglich beeinflusst werden durfte. Gleichzeitig aber sollte die Landschaft in weitem Maße integriert werden. Die natürliche Neigung wurde bei der Planung berücksichtigt und man schuf eine unterirdische Struktur mit wenig Außenflächen, die ausgezeichnet die Wärme speichert. Das Dach ist eine Art Fortsetzung des Geländes, das das Gebäude vollständig tarnt und als Wärmedämmung dient. Die Schlafzimmer liegen unterirdisch und werden durch schräge Schächte beleuchtet, durch die Tageslicht in verschiedenen Winkeln einfällt. Alle Oberflächen sind aus Holz. Der mittlere Bereich der Wohnung ist sehr vielseitig und die Wohn- und Schlafzimmer können je nach den Anforderungen der Bewohner verteilt werden. Um mehr Lagerraum zu schaffen, wurden in den Zwischen- und Seitenwänden Schränke eingelassen.

The roof is an extension of the terrain, providing the building with camouflage cover and thermal insulation.

La toiture est un prolongement du terrain, camouflant ainsi l'édifice dans sa quasi totalité et l'isolant sur le plan thermique.

Das Dach ist wie eine Fortsetzung des Geländes, das das Gebäude vollständig tarnt und als Wärmedämmung dient.

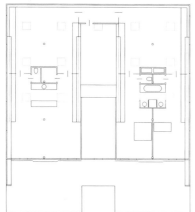

› Plan Plan Grundriss

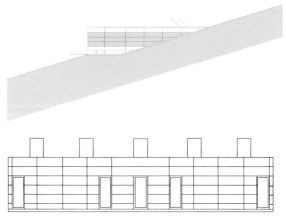

› Elevations Élévations Aufrisse

All the finishing is of wood. Most of the prefabricated units were assembled by the owners.

Tous les finis intérieurs sont en bois : la plupart, composés de pièces préfabriquées, ont été assemblés par les propriétaires.

Alle Oberflächen im Inneren sind aus Holz, die meisten davon sind vorgefertigte Teile, die von den Besitzern selbst zusammengebaut wurden.

Villa Deys

This house, situated close to the Rhine marshes, was designed for a couple who wished to live as independently as possible. Completely at one with the surrounding natural environment, the house has technical resources that allow the inhabitants to be self-sufficient. Instead of conventional doorways, the architects installed electronic sliding doors, operated by a remote control, which also opens and closes the front door, curtains and sunlight filters. The interior swimming pool is not very deep and is maintained at a constant temperature; the polished glass surfaces surrounding the pool set up views of the exterior. The lighting is programmed so that different switches activate various lighting schemes, depending on requirements: reading, resting or eating.

Cette habitation, située près des marais du Rhin, est conçue par un couple qui voulait habiter de manière la plus indépendante possible. Entièrement intégrée à la nature qui l'entoure, la maison dispose de moyens techniques permettant à ses habitants d'être autosuffisants. A la place de portes ordinaires, les architectes ont installé des portes coulissantes électroniques télécommandées qui ouvrent et ferment également les rideaux, la porte d'entrée et les filtres solaires. La piscine intérieure, peu profonde, se maintient à une température constante et les parois de verre poli, qui l'entourent, permettent de jouir des vues extérieures. Les lumières sont programmées pour que divers interrupteurs actionnent des types d'éclairage, variant selon les besoins : lire, se reposer ou dîner.

Dieses Haus in der Nähe der Stauseen am Rhein wurde für ein Paar entworfen, das so autonom wie möglich wohnen wollte. Es fügt sich vollkommen in die Natur der Umgebung ein und ist mit den notwendigen technischen Mitteln ausgestattet, durch die die Bewohner selbstgenügsam leben können. Statt normaler Türen wurden elektronische Schiebetüren eingebaut, die durch eine Fernbedienung geöffnet und geschlossen werden können. Auch die Gardinen, die Eingangstür und die Sonnenfilter werden über die Fernbedienung gesteuert. Der Swimmingpool im Haus ist nicht besonders tief und hält stets die gleiche Wassertemperatur. Die Wände aus poliertem Glas, die ihn umgeben, lassen den Blick nach draußen frei. Die Lampen sind so programmiert, dass über verschiedene Schalter verschiedene Beleuchtungskörper aktiviert werden können, je nachdem, ob man lesen, sich entspannen oder zu Abend essen will.

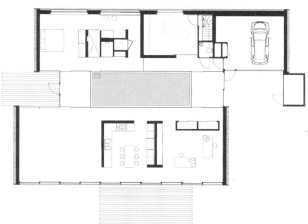

› Ground floor Rez-de-chaussée Erdgeschoss

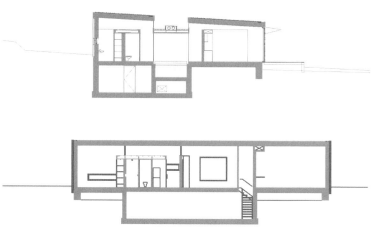

› Sections Sections Schnitte

The electronic sliding doors, curtains, front door and sunlight filters are operated by remote control.

Les architectes ont installé des portes coulissantes électroniques télécommandées qui ouvrent et ferment également les rideaux, la porte d'entrée et les filtres solaires.

Es wurden elektronische Schiebetüren eingebaut, die genau wie die Gardinen, die Eingangstür und die Sonnenfilter durch eine Fernbedienung geöffnet und geschlossen werden.

The indoor pool is shallow and maintained at a constant temperature. The polished glass surfaces surrounding the pool offer views to the exterior.

La piscine intérieure, peu profonde, se maintient à une température constante. Les murs de verre poli, qui l'entourent, permettent de jouir des vues sur l'extérieur.

Der Swimmingpool im Haus ist nicht sehr tief und hält eine konstante Temperatur. Die Wände aus poliertem Glas, die ihn umgeben, lassen den Blick nach draußen frei.

Two Houses in Ponte de Lima
Deux maisons à Ponte de Lima
Zwei Häuser in Ponte de Lima

These two buildings give the impression of having been hollowed out of the landscape to form a dynamic composition of geometrical lines and angular surfaces which challenges the conventions of contemporary, minimalist architecture. Situated on a steep hillside, the volumes maintain a constant architectural dialog and integrate perfectly into the environment. The inclined structure which encloses the interior spaces also creates a shaded outdoor patio. The lighting provided by the glass doors and skylights is heightened by the neutrality of the interior color scheme. Spectacular views can be enjoyed from within the house, which looks out over the expansive surrounding landscape.

Ces deux habitations semblent avoir été creusées dans le paysage pour former une composition dynamique aux lignes géométriques et aux surfaces anguleuses défiant les idées conventionnelles de l'architecture contemporaine et minimaliste. Situés à la cime d'une colline, les volumes maintiennent un dialogue architectural constant et s'intègrent parfaitement à l'environnement. La structure inclinée, qui enveloppe les espaces intérieurs, crée un patio extérieur ombragé. La lumière apportée par les portes en verre et par les lucarnes est maximalisée par les tons neutres des intérieurs. Depuis les chambres, les vues sur l'immensité du paysage environnant, sont spectaculaires.

Diese beiden Häuser wirken, als ob sie in die Landschaft gegraben sind, um eine dynamische Komposition aus geometrischen Linien und eckigen Flächen zu bilden, die die konventionellen Aspekte der zeitgenössischen und minimalistischen Architektur herausfordern. Sie liegen an einem steilen Hang. Die beiden Formen scheinen in einem ständigen, architektonischen Dialog zu stehen und sie integrieren sich perfekt in ihre Umgebung. Die geneigte Struktur, die die Räume umhüllt, schafft einen schattigen Hof. Das Licht, das durch die Glastüren und die Dachfenster fällt, wird durch die neutralen Farben der Räume noch unterstrichen. Von diesen Häusern aus hat man einen wundervollen Blick auf die weite Landschaft der Umgebung.

The lighting provided by the glass doors and skylights is heightened by the neutrality of the interior color scheme.

L'éclairage, obtenu par les portes tout en verre et les lucarnes, est maximalisé par les tons neutres des intérieurs.

Das Licht, das durch die Glastüren und die Dachfenster fällt, wird durch die neutralen Farben der Räume noch verstärkt.

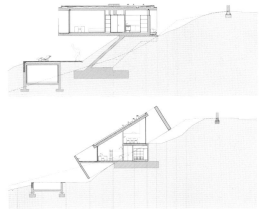

› Ground floor Rez-de-chaussée Erdgeschoss   › First floor Premier étage Erstes Obergeschoss   › Sections Sections Schnitte

Möbius House
Maison Möbius
Möbiushaus

Möbius House embodies a new vision of the private home, where spaces are loosely linked, with no clear boundaries limiting the rooms. At times, these vague spatial limits coincide with those affecting the functional and temporal aspects of the activities pursued within. The house interweaves every different use in a spiralling design of work, social activities, family life and individual living patterns. The basic scheme comprises two itineraries that converge in the marginal spaces, demonstrating how two people can live together sharing certain communal spaces without giving up their independence. This concept relies on the use of concrete and glass, the two building materials used throughout in alternate applications. In this highly sophisticated project, scenarios are created where form, function and time fuse together to give rise to separate and attractive environments.

La maison Möbius est une nouvelle approche de l'habitation privée : les espaces se succèdent sans créer de limites claires entre les pièces, limites comprenant également celles qui affectent la fonctionnalité et la temporalité des actions réalisées à l'intérieur. La maison relie et entrelace toutes les activités de l'habitation, conciliant travail, vie sociale, vie familiale et vie individuelle au sein de son design en spirale. Le diagramme constitutif inclut deux trajectoires linéaires fermées convergeant dans des espaces marginaux, et prouve que deux personnes peuvent vivre ensemble sans perdre leur indépendance tout en partageant certains espaces communs. Ce concept touche l'organisation des deux matériaux de base employés à la construction de l'habitation: béton et verre, interchangeables selon les fonctions. Le projet est un design sophistiqué, doté de scénarios capables de mettre en relation la forme, la fonction et le temps, tout en créant des ambiances chaleureuses et séparées.

Das Möbiushaus ist eine neue Art und Weise, das Privathaus zu verstehen. Die Räume gehen ineinander über, ohne dass es klare Grenzen zwischen den Zimmern gibt. Das Haus verbindet und verknüpft alle Aktivitäten in seiner Raumgestaltung miteinander: die Arbeit, das gesellschaftliche Leben, das Familienleben und das Leben der einzelnen Personen. Das grundlegende Schema enthält zwei geschlossene, lineare Bahnen, die in den Räumen am Rand zusammenfließen. Es zeigt, wie zwei Personen zusammenleben können, ohne dabei ihre Unabhängigkeit zu verlieren, und gleichzeitig bestimmte gemeinsame Bereiche teilen können. Dieses Konzept betrifft die Organisation der wichtigsten verwendeten Baustoffe: Zement und Glas, deren Anwendungen ausgetauscht werden. Es handelt sich um hoch entwickelte Szenarios, die dazu dienen, die Form, die Funktion und die Zeit miteinander in Verbindung zu setzen, und gleichzeitig warme und einzigartige Umgebungen zu schaffen.

All the structural elements are of concrete, with fully glazed intermediate spaces. As a result, the building offers a light, transparent appearance.

Tous les éléments porteurs sont en ciment et sont agrémentés de grandes baies vitrées, conférant à l'édifice légèreté et transparence.

Alle tragenden Elemente bestehen aus Zement und werden durch große Glasfenster ergänzt. So wirkt das Gebäude leicht und transparent.

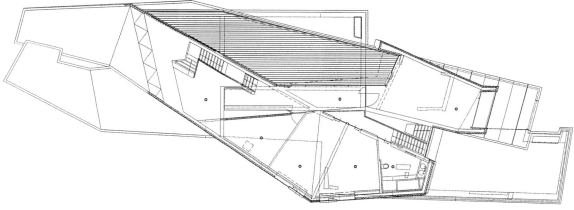

› Plan Plan Grundriss

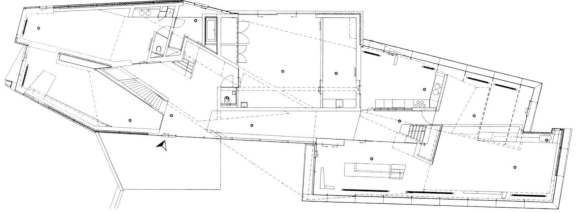

› Plan Plan Grundriss

Plastic House
Maison de plastique
Kunststoffhaus

Concrete is undoubtedly one of the most extensively used construction materials of the 20th century, and its ease of use and great durability make it the universal construction material par excellence. In this project, a house built for a successful photographer and his family, the architect proposed a new relationship with the environment through the use of a different material: polyurethane reinforced with glass fiber. This consists of a 4 mm layer of injected plastic, in various shapes and sizes, which, owing to the quality of its fibers, may take on the appearance of anything from paper to bamboo. The external walls, terraces, staircases and dividing walls are all made from this material, which transforms the house into a palace of gently screened luminosity. The plastic house's fitness for human habitation is considered from the perspective of the building materials rather than the layout, since the material communicates with our body through every detail.

Le béton, sans aucun doute un des matériaux les plus employés du XXe siècle, devient, par son emploi facile et sa haute résistance, l'élément de construction par excellence. Dans ce projet, une maison pour un grand photographe et sa famille, l'architecte propose de créer une relation nouvelle avec l'environnement en utilisant un matériel différent : le FRP (polyuréthanne renforcé de fibres de verre). Il s'agit de plastique injecté de 4 mm d'épaisseur, de différentes formes et gabarits et qui, dû à la qualité de ses fibres, ressemble parfois à du papier ou à du bambou. Les murs extérieurs, les terrasses, les escaliers et les cloisons sont en FRP, ce qui transforme la maison en un cube de lumière irradiant une luminosité douce et tamisée. L'habitabilité de la maison de plastique est étudiée à partir des matériaux de revêtement plutôt qu'à partir de la distribution, pour que la matière dialogue avec notre corps par le biais de chaque détail.

Eines der meistverwendeten Materialien des 20. Jh. ist zweifelsohne der Beton. Aufgrund seiner einfachen Anwendung und großen Festigkeit wurde er zu einem erstklassigen Konstruktionsmittel. Dieses Haus, das für einen bekannten Fotografen und seine Familie errichtet wurde, schafft eine neue Beziehung zur Umwelt durch die Benutzung eines anderen Materials, nämlich PU (glasfaserverstärktes Polyurethan). Es handelt sich um 4 mm dicken Spritzkunststoff in verschiedenen Formen und Größen, der aufgrund der Qualität der Fasern manchmal wie Papier und manchmal wie Bambus aussieht. Die Außenmauern der Terrasse, die Treppen und die Zwischenwände sind aus PU, was das Haus zu einem Lichtkasten macht, der ein feines und gedämpftes Licht ausstrahlt. Die Bewohnbarkeit dieses Kunststoffhauses beruht auf der Materialqualität der Verkleidung und nicht auf der Aufteilung, wei dieses Material in jedem Detail mit unserem Körper in Kommunikation steht.

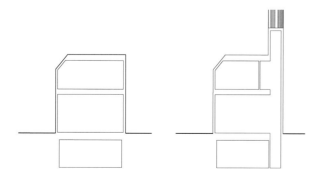

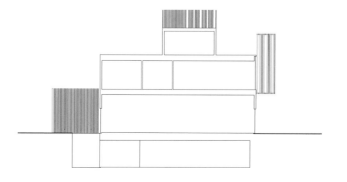

› Sections Sections Schnitte

Great care has been taken to ensure that every detail safeguards the distinctive qualities of each material.

Les détails ont été conçus avec une attention particulière pour maintenir l'originalité de chaque matériau.

Die Einzelheiten wurden besonders sorgfältig gestaltet, um die Einzigartigkeit jedes Materials zu unterstreichen.

0|8

This team, leaded by Hiroyuki Arima, projected a single building with an array of spaces on five, totally white levels. The commission presented a certain degree of difficulty, since the young owners had a lengthy list of requirements. From a conceptual point of view, contemporary solutions are provided for each different use, within the small amount of space available. Rooms are partitioned off in accordance with the intended activities, classified on a scale of 0 to 8. Some were conceived in accordance with the desires and individual personalities of the resident couple. The architects sought to explore the possibilities opened up by the interior, while making sure that the layout of the rooms did not conform to any hierarchical pattern. Thus, two fundamental objectives were met: rich spaces and pure volumes.

Cette équipe, dirigée par Hiroyuki Arima, a projeté un édifice unique avec une succession d'espaces répartis sur cinq niveaux totalement blancs. Le programme n'était pas simple à réaliser, car il devait intégrer une longue liste d'exigences requises par la jeune propriétaire. La conception de l'ensemble a fait usage d'idées contemporaines pour définir les différentes fonctions de l'espace réduit. La division des pièces s'est faite selon les activités qui devaient avoir lieu à l'intérieur, en suivant un classement de 0 à 8. Certaines ont été conçues en tenant compte des idées du couple, tout en considérant l'individualité et l'originalité des résidents. Les architectes voulaient explorer les possibilités offertes par l'intérieur et une partie du travail était d'assurer que la distribution des pièces ne se fasse pas selon une distribution hiérarchique. Deux objectifs de base ont pu ainsi être atteints : richesse des espaces et volumes aux lignes pures.

Das Team, unter der Leitung von Hiroyuki Arima, entwarf ein Gebäude mit einer gegliederten Aufeinanderfolge von Räumen auf fünf absolut weißen Ebenen. Es gab bei diesem Auftrag gewisse Schwierigkeiten, weil das junge Paar, dem das Gebäude gehört, sehr viele Anforderungen stellte. Das Konzept basiert auf zeitgenössischen Formeln, die dabei helfen, die verschiedenen Nutzungen des relativ kleinen Raums zu definieren. Die Räume werden je nach den Aktivitäten, die darin stattfinden, aufgeteilt, und von 0 bis 8 eingeteilt. Einige davon wurden unter der Berücksichtigung der Tatsache gestaltet, dass es sich um ein Paar handelt, aber gleichzeitig auch um zwei einzigartige Personen. Die Architekten hatten die Absicht, das Potential der Räume zu erforschen und ein Teil dieser Aufgabe bestand darin, sicherzustellen, dass die Räume nicht hierarchisch angeordnet sind. So wurden zwei grundlegende Ziele erreicht: man schuf reiche Räume und Formen mit klaren Linien.

Wooden floors in pale tones harmonize with the white walls to create a peaceful atmosphere.

Les sols sont en bois clair et se marient avec les murs blancs, créant une ambiance de tranquillité et de paix.

Die Böden sind aus hellem Holz, das gut zu den weißen Wänden passt. Es entsteht eine Atmosphäre der Ruhe und des Friedens.

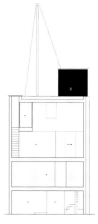

› Section Section Schnitt

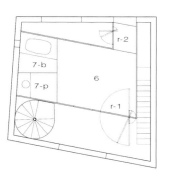

› Plan Plan Grundriss

The lightweight spiral staircase provides access to the upper floors.

L'escalier en colimaçon, construit en matériaux légers, permet d'accéder aux niveaux supérieurs.

Die Wendeltreppe ist aus leichtem Material und führt in die oberen Etagen.

THE GRID 72-78 BAYSWATER ROAD

The Grid

Le quadrillage

Schachbrett

This seven-story building on a gently sloping street owes its name to its checkerboard pattern of cubes and straight lines. The concise sobriety of the design stands out as the main feature in this attractive, medium-sized housing complex. Its structure, made from large, prefabricated concrete wall panels and Ultrafloor slabs, recreates the checkerboard structure visible on the north elevation, where each home is clearly discernible as a rectangular tube on a north-south axis. The two attic homes are built on light steel structures with a large rooftop terrace on either side. The master bedrooms open onto an interior patio, separated from the hall by sliding translucent glass doors. At night, the interiors shine through to the exterior, illuminating the ponds at the base of the lightwells.

Cet édifice de sept étages, situé dans une rue légèrement en pente, doit son nom au design en forme de quadrillage et à sa composition symétrique de formes linéaires. Un design concis et sobre caractérise cet intéressant complexe d'habitations de taille modeste. La structure se compose de grands panneaux muraux de béton préfabriqué et de plaques d'Ultrafloor à la base de la simple structure en quadrillage visible sur l'élévation nord, dans laquelle chaque habitation se présente comme un tube rectangulaire allant du nord au sud. Les deux attiques sont des structures d'acier léger flanquées de grandes terrasses. Un patio intérieur communique avec la chambre à coucher des maîtres et est séparé du vestibule par des portes coulissantes de verre transparent. De nuit, les intérieurs éclairés animent l'extérieur de l'édifice et permettent de voir deux étangs situés à la base des foyers d'éclairage.

Dieses siebenstöckige Gebäude liegt auf einer leicht abschüssigen Straße. Es verdankt seinen Namen der Karoform und der symmetrischen Komposition, die aus Würfeln und linearen Formen besteht. Die konzise und schlichte Gestaltung charakterisiert diesen attraktiven, nicht allzu großen Wohnungsblock. Die Struktur besteht aus großen, vorgefertigten Wandpaneelen aus Beton und Platten der Marke Ultrafloor, die eine einfache Struktur mit einem Karomuster schaffen, das man an der Nordhöhe erkennen kann, an der jede Wohnung wie ein rechteckiges Rohr vom Norden nach Süden angeordnet ist. Die beiden Dachwohnungen sind aus Leichtmetall, und an ihren Seiten grenzen große Terrassen an. Ein Innenhof schafft eine Verbindung zum Schlafzimmer. Er ist durch Schiebetüren aus transparentem Glas von der Diele abgetrennt. Nachts beleben die beleuchteten Wohnungen die Fassade des Gebäudes und man sieht die beiden Wasserbecken in den Hohlräumen der Beleuchtung.

Despite the open-plan interior, movable panels can be used to close off different zones temporarily.

Bien que l'intérieur soit organisé à partir d'un plan complètement ouvert, des panneaux amovibles peuvent séparer temporairement les zones.

Obwohl das Innere völlig offen organisiert ist, kann man mit beweglichen Paneelen zeitweise bestimmte Bereiche absondern.

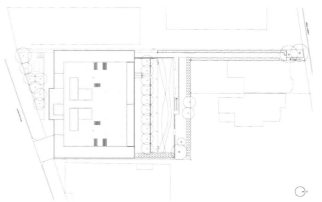

› Location plan Plan de situation Umgebungsplan

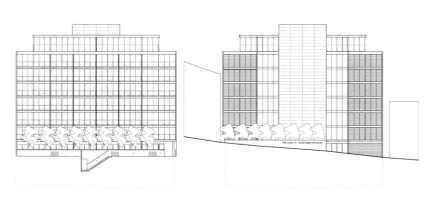

› Elevations Élévations Aufrisse

Glass House
Maison de verre
Glashaus

The repetition of a basic module the size of an ordinary bedroom determines the structure, overall layout of space, and the rhythm governing the openings on to the exterior. Within such a minimalist framework, the program of requirements is easily met, since it is fully compatible with conventional uses and affects the entire building, including the exterior. On the main façade and two sides of the building, a protective outer skin of printed glass conceals the dimensions and position of the windows in the inner wall. The small entrance porch and garage door are the only interruptions in this glazed wrapping, causing the front door to stand out with great definition. During the daytime, this glass barrier reflects the space around it like a mirror; at night, however, artificial lighting reveals the environment within. The elegant structure, strict modular scheme and strong minimalist tendencies add the final aesthetic touches to this small building.

Le projet est basé sur la répétition d'un module de la taille d'une simple chambre à coucher, déterminant à la fois la structure et la distribution de l'espace et le rythme de composition des ouvertures. Ce cadre minimaliste est en harmonie avec le programme, qu'il intègre de manière conventionnelle presque sans variations, tout en dominant aussi l'extérieur. En direction de la rue et des façades latérales, une plaque de verre gravé, suspendue à l'instar d'une aile de ventilateur, protége le volume tout en masquant la taille et la position des ouvertures. Seul le petit porche d'entrée et la porte du garage brisent la continuité de la toiture et définissent clairement l'entrée. De jour, le pan de verre reflète l'espace environnant, à l'instar d'un miroir et de nuit, l'éclairage révèle le monde intérieur de la maison. La structure élégante, la modulation rigoureuse et un certain aspect minimaliste parachèvent l'image de ce petit édifice.

Die Gebäudestruktur beruht auf der Wiederholung eines Moduls der Größe eines einfachen Schlafzimmers, die nicht nur die Form bestimmt, sondern auch die Aufteilung des Raumes. Die Wohnfunktionen fügen sich sehr gut in diesen minimalistischen Rahmen ein. Sie konnten auf konventionelle Weise umgesetzt werden und erstrecken sich bis nach draußen. Zur Straße und den Seitenfassaden hin wurde eine gravierte Glasplatte montiert, die wie der Flügel eines Ventilators aufgehängt wurde, und so das Haus beschützt und die Größe und Position der Öffnungen verbirgt. Nur die kleine Vorhalle am Eingang und die Garagentür unterbrechen die Kontinuität des Daches und definieren auf klare Weise den Eingangsbereich. Tagsüber reflektiert die verglaste Ebene die Umgebung, so als ob es sich um einen Spiegel handelte, und nachts bescheint das Licht von innen das Haus. Die elegante Struktur, die strenge Modulation und der minimalistische Touch vervollständigen das Gesamtbild dieses kleinen Gebäudes.

The material covering the main façade reflects the colors and shadows of the natural surroundings, allowing the house to melt into the landscape.

Le matériau de revêtement de la façade reflète les couleurs et les ombres de la nature et permet à la maison de s'intégrer directement à l'environnement.

Das Material, mit dem die Fassade verkleidet ist, reflektiert die Farben und Schatten der Natur. So fügt sich das Haus diskret in die Umgebung ein.

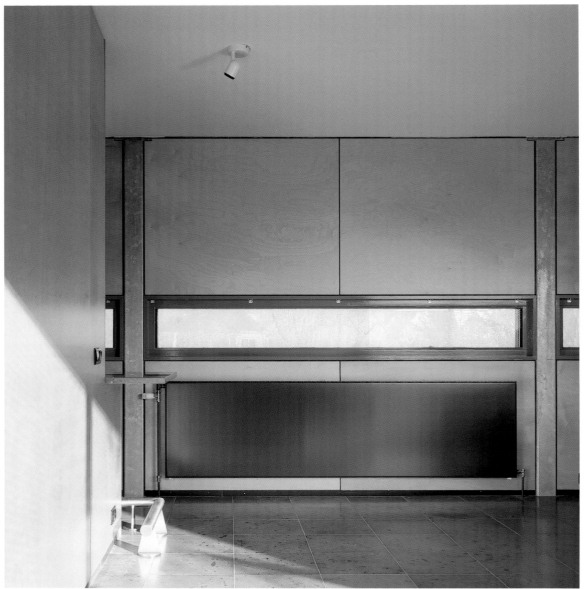

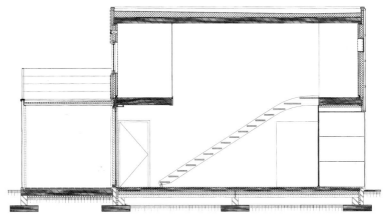

› Section Section Schnitt

Residence in Fukuoka
Résidence à Fukuoka
Haus in Fukuoka

The underlying idea for this project was to raise the home above the ground and wrap it in cloth, thus eliminating the notion of "walls" altogether and using, instead, a translucent membrane that alters its color with the changing light falling on it during the course of the day. This material is sandwiched between two panes of transparent glass. From the exterior, the result resembles a floating box of lights. On the inside, an effect of great depth is achieved, since there are no walls to close off the house's outer shell. A passage running parallel to the transparent partition doubles as a hall, its narrow dimensions and low ceiling contrasting with the rest of the interior, which appears larger that it really is. This strategye, playing with scale is applied again on the other division, where a small space, just three feet wide by 30 ft long, contains a patio with a tree growing through the wooden deck.

Le projet est né de l'idée d'élever l'habitation du sol et de l'envelopper d'un tissage, détrônant le concept de mur et le remplaçant par une membrane translucide changeant de couleur au gré des variations de lumière du jour. Cette membrane est enfermée entre deux feuilles de verre qui, en elles-mêmes, sont transparentes. L'impression, qui émane de l'extérieur, est celle d'une boîte de lumières s'élevant, tandis que l'intérieur dégage une forte impression de profondeur, vu qu'aucun mur ne ferme les quatre côtés de l'habitation. Un couloir qui court parallèlement au mur translucide sert d'antichambre à l'habitation; son étroitesse et son toit bas établissent un contrepoint avec l'intérieur, qui parait plus grand de ce qu'il est en réalité. Cette stratégie de changement d'échelle s'applique sur l'autre mur, où un espace d'à peine un mètre de large et de neuf de long permet de créer un petit patio avec un arbre qui sort du sol en bois.

Dieses Projekt entstand aus der Idee heraus, die Wohnung über den Boden zu heben und mit einem Gewebe zu umwickeln, um so das Konzept der Wand zu verändern und sie durch eine lichtdurchlässige Membran zu ersetzen, deren Farbe sich je nach den Lichtverhältnissen zu jeder Tageszeit ändert. Diese Membran wird von zwei Glasflügeln umschlossen, die für sich allein transparent sind. Von außen hat man den Eindruck, dass es sich um einen schwebenden Lichtkasten handelt, während das Innere sehr tief wirkt, da es keine Wand an den vier Seiten der Wohnung gibt. Ein Flur, der als Vorzimmer der Wohnung dient, verläuft parallel zu der durchscheinenden Wand. Seine niedrige Decke setzt einen Kontrapunkt zum Inneren, das größer wirkt als es wirklich ist. Diese Strategie der Veränderung der Größe wurde auch an einer anderen Wand angewendet, wo man einen knapp einen Meter breiten, neun Meter langen Raum abgetrennt hat, um einen kleinen Hof zu schaffen, in dem ein Baum auf dem Holzboden wächst.

A translucent structure alters its color with the changing light falling on it during the course of the day.

Une structure cubique translucide change de couleur selon les variations de lumière au fil de la journée.

Eine kubische, durchscheinende Struktur verändert die Farbe mit den wechselnden Lichtverhältnissen im Tagesverlauf.

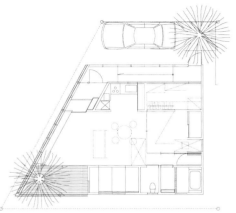

› Ground floor Rez-de-chaussée Erdgeschoss

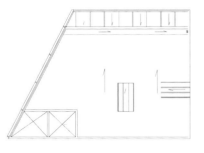

› First floor Premier étage Erstes Obergeschoss

S.H.

Located on a hill in a quiet neighborhood, this house belongs to a married couple. Its height compensates for the narrowness of the plot, making interior relatively spacious. The interior space comprises five stories spread over two levels. It was conceived as one enormous unit, arranged in such a way that privacy gradually increased on the upper floors. The overall living space cannot be viewed in its entirety from any one position: this mini-house indisputably makes the most of its height and capacity. The most private area is contained inside a sort of white box, which is formed from a series of window openings designed according to the owner's wishes, taking into account the surroundings. Even though the site is narrow, the exterior area enjoys an exceedingly warm atmosphere.

Située sur une colline, dans un environnement calme, cette habitation appartient à un couple. La hauteur de la maison compense l'étroitesse du terrain, si bien que l'intérieur est assez large. Cinq étages, articulés sur deux niveaux, configurent l'espace intérieur, conçu comme une immense habitation. L'intimité augmente au fur et à mesure que l'on accède aux niveaux supérieurs. Aucun angle ne permet de voir l'espace entier : c'est sans aucun doute une mini maison originale, exploitant au maximum sa hauteur et son volume. Une espèce de boite blanche, contenant l'espace plus privé, est formé d'une série de fenêtres créées en fonction de l'environnement et des désirs du client. Malgré l'étroitesse du terrain, la zone extérieure jouit d'une atmosphère extrêmement chaleureuse.

Dieses Haus im Besitz eines Ehepaars liegt auf einem Hügel in einer ruhigen Nachbarschaft. Da das Grundstück sehr klein ist, baute man ein hohes Haus, wodurch im Inneren relativ viel Platz entstand. Der Innenraum, der wie ein einziger, riesiger Raum verstanden wurde, besteht aus fünf Erhebungen auf zwei Ebenen, so dass allmählich mehr Privatsphäre entsteht, je höher man geht. Es gibt keinen Winkel, von dem aus man den kompletten Raum überschauen kann. Es handelt sich ganz ohne Zweifel um ein sehr originelles Minihaus, in dem die Höhe und Form maximal ausgenutzt wurden. Die privatesten Räume befinden sich in einer Art weißem Kasten, der durch eine Reihe von Fensteröffnungen geformt wird, die auf Wunsch des Eigentümers entworfen wurden, aber auch von der Umgebung beeinflusst sind. Obwohl das Grundstück sehr klein ist, gibt es dennoch attraktive Außenanlagen.

This house has four staircases; their slope becomes less pronounced on the higher levels, in order to convey a greater sense of intimacy.

La maison possède un total de quatre escaliers : au fur et à mesure de la montée, l'angle est moins prononcé, à la faveur de l'intimité des zones supérieures.

In dem Haus gibt es insgesamt vier Treppen, und wenn man diese Treppen hochsteigt, wird der Winkel kleiner, so dass die oberen Stockwerke zurückgezogener wirken.

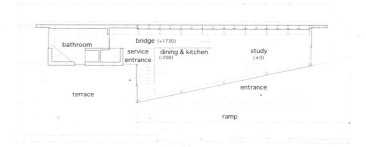

bathroom

bridge (+1730)

service
entrance

dining & kitchen
(-200)

study
(±0)

terrace

entrance

ramp

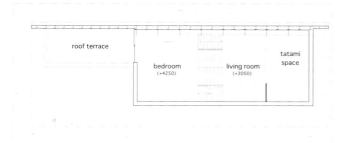

roof terrace

bedroom
(+4250)

living room
(+3050)

tatami
space

› Plans Plans Grundrisse

Sintra, Portugal | Anabela Leitão, Daiji Kondo

House in Beloura
Maison à Beloura
Haus in Beloura

The client established a series of conditions for the construction of this house on a south-facing lot: an indoor pool, a minimum of communicating spaces and natural light in every room. In order to ensure the project fulfilled all these aims, the architects designed a compact block with a stairwell in its center, so that all the rooms look out on the exterior. The interior space was arranged on seven tiered levels, to make full use of the available space and preserve a sense of continuity throughout. The living room, devoid of a ceiling, enjoys visual contact with the library and the staircase, which defines the limits of each new level. The ground floor has been designed to reflect this multidirectional light against a variety of carefully selected materials. Each room, including the kitchen and the bathrooms, has been painstakingly designed to the very last detail.

Dans ce projet, le client a établit une série de conditions préalables à la construction de l'habitation, située sur une parcelle orientée sud : une piscine intérieure, un nombre réduit d'espaces communicants et la lumière naturelle dans toutes les pièces. Pour atteindre les objectifs en question, les architectes ont conçu un bloc compact avec un escalier comme axe central, permettant à toutes les chambres de regarder vers l'extérieur. L'intérieur s'organise autour de sept demi niveaux pour optimaliser les espaces et transmettre une impression de fluidité continue. Le toit du salon disparaît pour créer un lien visuel entre la bibliothèque et l'escalier, délimitant les niveaux de chaque palier. L'intérieur du rez-de-chaussée a été conçu en une variété de matériaux pour refléter cette lumière allant dans toutes les directions : toutes les pièces ont été étudiées avec le même soin méticuleux du détail, y compris la cuisine et les salles de bains.

Der Kunde, der sich dieses Haus auf einem Grundstück in Südlage bauen ließ, hatte eine Reihe von Wünschen und Anforderungen. Er wollte einen Swimmingpool im Haus, wenig Verbindungsräume und viel Tageslicht in allen Räumen. Um diesen Anforderungen gerecht zu werden, entwarfen die Architekten einen kompakten Block mit einer Treppe als Mittelpunkt, so dass alle Zimmer nach außen liegen. Die Innenräume sind in sieben Halbgeschosse aufgeteilt, wodurch der Raum optimal genutzt wird und ein Gefühl von Stetigkeit entsteht. Die Decke des Wohnzimmers verschwindet und es entsteht eine visuelle Verbindung zwischen der Bibliothek und der Treppe, die die Grenzen zu jedem Geschoss definiert. Das Erdgeschoss wurde so entworfen, dass das Licht durch verschiedene Materialien in alle Richtungen reflektiert wird. Bei allen Räumen, einschließlich Küche und Bad, wurde die gleiche Sorgfalt und Methodik angewandt und auch die kleinste Einzelheit sorgsam durchdacht.

Openings in the rectangular design accommodate balconies at different heights throughout the home, deliberately placed to take full advantage of the best views over the garden.

Les renfoncements dans les blocs rectangulaires de la maison accueillent des balcons situés à différentes hauteurs, conçus pour profiter au maximum des vues sur le jardin.

Die Hohlräume in den rechteckigen Blöcken des Hauses bilden Balkone auf verschiedenen Höhen, von denen aus man einen schönen Blick auf den Garten hat.

276

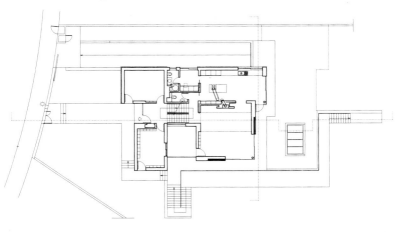

› Plan Plan Grundriss

White Ribbing House

Habitation White Ribbing

Haus White Ribbing

Building a secluded haven of tranquillity in bustling downtown Tokyo is, to say the least, a tall order. The team at Milligram Studio have achieved such a feat with this rather unusual house, built on a rectangular ground plan. The façade is deliberately left free of detail, and the project displays strictly formal architecture, based on open spaces and well-illuminated interiors. The pentagonal shape encloses a pure, balanced interior, where light encounters white walls to enhance a sense of spaciousness. The rooms are very open and carefully arranged to create a clean-cut, flowing environment. The irregular roof structure gives the top floor a unique attic-like character. White Ribbing has all the expressive power sought by many contemporary family homes. It is an attractive design with a flexible, fluent interior.

Construire un havre de paix au coeur d'une ville aussi frénétique que Tokyo est, sans aucun doute, un pari difficile. L'équipe du Milligram Studio l'a pourtant gagné en créant cette habitation irrégulière construite sur un plan de base rectangulaire. Le design de la façade du projet est dépourvu de détails. L'architecture, strictement formelle, se compose d'espaces ouverts et d'intérieurs clairs. La forme pentagonale enferme un intérieur pur et équilibré où la lumière se fond avec les murs blancs pour créer une impression d'amplitude. Les différentes pièces sont très ouvertes et sont disposées avec soin pour créer un environnement pur et fluide. La structure irrégulière de la toiture confère à l'étage supérieur une sensation unique, similaire à celle d'un attique. White Ribbing a une force d'expression à laquelle nombre d'habitations individuelles contemporaines aspirent. Il s'agit d'un design intéressant avec un intérieur modulable et fluide.

Eine Oase des Friedens im Zentrum einer so frenetischen Stadt wie Tokio zu schaffen ist ohne Zweifel eine schwierige Herausforderung. Das Team von Milligram Studio erreichte dieses Ziel mit einem recht ungewöhnlichen Haus, das auf einer ebenen Fläche mit rechteckigem Grundriss errichtet wurde. Bei der Gestaltung der Fassade verzichtete man auf überflüssige Einzelheiten. Die Architektur ist streng formal und basiert auf offenen Räumen und hellen Umgebungen. Die fünfeckige Form umschließt eine reine und ausgeglichene Wohnumgebung, in der das Licht mit den weißen Wänden verschmilzt und so den Eindruck von Weite schafft. Die verschiedenen Räume sind offen und sehr sorgfältig angeordnet, um eine saubere und fließende Umgebung zu schaffen. White Ribbing hat eine Ausdruckskraft, die viele der zeitgenössischen Einfamilienhäuser anstreben. Es handelt sich um eine sehr ansprechende Gestaltung mit einem flexiblen und flüssigen Innenraum.

White floors and walls reflect the light entering through the large windows and the skylight, resulting in an extremely bright space.

Les sols et murs blancs reflètent la lumière qui entre par les grandes fenêtres et la lucarne, créant un espace extraordinairement lumineux.

Die weißen Böden und Wände reflektieren das Licht, das durch die großen Fenster und das Dachfenster fällt, so dass ein außerordentlich heller Raum entsteht.

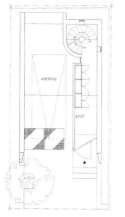

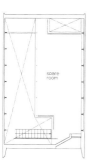

› Plans Plans Grundrisse

AYM House
Habitation AYM
Haus AYM

This house in one of the pedestrian precincts in the northern district of Valencia is a magnificent example of integration with the historical context. Outside, it presents respectful proportions and dimensions, but these hide a contemporary house focused around a patio. The façade presents two vertical Climalit glass windows, crowned by a small metal parapet that breaks the symmetry. The entrance is next to a blind doorway with darkened glass, which suggests the internal design of the house. An oblique staircase separates the service areas, adjacent to the street, from the open plan rooms giving on to the patio, creating four separate spaces with sliding doors hidden inside the furnishings. Light radiates upward from the ground floor, gradually intensifying as it approaches the attic.

Cette maison, située dans un quartier des rues piétonnes du nord de Valence, est un magnifique exemple d'intégration dans le contexte historique. L'aspect extérieur, aux mesures et proportions respectueuses, recèle une habitation contemporaine tournée vers le patio. La façade présente deux fenêtres dotées de verre Climalit alignées verticalement, terminées par un petit rebord métallique qui rompt la symétrie. L'accès est adjacent au mur mitoyen, à côté d'un portique fermé aux verres opaques dévoilant l'ambiance intérieure de la maison. Un escalier transversal sépare les zones de service qui donnent sur la rue, des pièces ouvertes vers le patio, définissant ainsi quatre espaces uniques intégrés grâce à des portes coulissantes cachées dans le mobilier. Le flux de lumière va du sous-sol au grenier, s'amplifiant au fil des étages.

Dieses Haus in einer Fußgängerzone im Norden Valencias ist ein wunderbares Beispiel für die Integration eines Gebäudes in das historische Umfeld. Von außen wurden die Formen und Maße an die Umgebung angepasst, aber innen betritt man eine zeitgenössische Wohnung, die sich zum Hof hin öffnet. An der Fassade sind zwei Fenster aus Glas der Marke Climalit, die vertikal ausgerichtet sind und eine kleine Brüstung aus Metall haben, die die Symmetrie unterbricht. Der Zugang liegt an der Trennmauer neben einem mit undurchsichtigem Glas verkleideten Portikus, der auf das Innere des Hauses schließen lässt. Eine schräge Treppe trennt die funktionellen Räume, die zur Straße hin liegen, von den offenen Räumen zum Hof ab und definiert vier verschiedene Bereiche, die durch schiebbare Wandschirme, die in den Möbeln verborgen sind, verbunden oder getrennt werden. Das Licht fällt vom Untergeschoss bis zum Dachboden ein, und wird nach oben immer stärker.

The mirror finish on the ground-floor tiles accentuates the luminosity permeating the entire design.

Le fini brillant du carrelage du rez-de-chaussée, tel un miroir, accentue la luminosité et la légèreté de l'ensemble.

Der glänzende Boden im Erdgeschoss, der wie ein Spiegel wirkt, sorgt für Helligkeit und wertet das Gesamtbild auf.

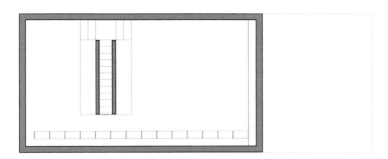

› Basement Sous-sol Kellergeschoss

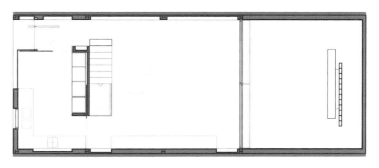

› Ground floor Rez-de-chaussée Erdgeschoss

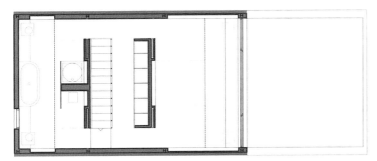

› First floor Premier étage Erstes Obergeschoss

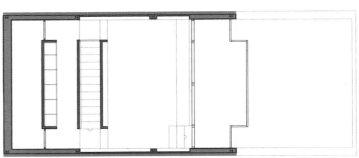

› Second floor Deuxième étage Zweites Obergeschoss

House in Uehonmachi

Maison à Uehonmachi

Haus in Uehonmachi

The outstanding longitudinal character of this house, located in Tennoji-ku, in the centre of the important city of Osaka, was chosen as the main feature to be emphasized. A thin glass screen divides the house from the street and the rear patio, whilst permitting adequate ventilation and lighting. The inside walls, made from reinforced concrete 140 mm thick, give structural solidity and presence to the living space on all floors. On the main façade, the steel structure is extended to support the balconies. The pillars, with a section 125 mm square and X-shape reinforcing ties, are strategically placed so as not to obstruct the line of sight. Inside, the sturdy pine flooring acts as an organic counterpoint to the steel, glass and concrete. Above all, this is a simple and efficient building, an exercise in the quest for what is truly essential in a home.

Dans cette habitation, située à Tennoji-ku, au cœur de la grande ville d'Osaka, l'idée première est d'exalter son caractère longitudinal. Une fine membrane de verre isole la maison de la rue et du patio arrière, tout en permettant une ventilation et un éclairage parfaits. Les murs mitoyens de béton précontraint de 140 mm d'épaisseur, confèrent solidité structurelle et présence à l'espace au fil des étages. Sur la façade principale, la structure d'acier se prolonge pour former les balcons. Les piliers à section carrée de 125x125 mm avec des tirants de soutien disposés en X, sont placés stratégiquement pour ne pas gêner la vue. A l'intérieur, le parquet en pin massif sert de contrepoint organique à l'acier, au verre et au béton. C'est avant tout, un édifice sobre et fonctionnel, un exercice de recherche sur ce qui est vraiment essentiel dans une habitation.

Bei diesem Haus in Tennoji-ku im Zentrum der Großstadt Osaka wollte man vor allem die längliche Form unterstreichen. Eine schmale Glasmembran trennt das Haus von der Straße und dem Hinterhof und sorgt für eine ausgezeichnete Belüftung und Beleuchtung. Die 140 mm dicken Zwischenmauern aus Spannbeton verleihen der Struktur Festigkeit und sorgen für bewohnbare Räume in der ganzen Wohnung. An der Hauptfassade wurde die Stahlstruktur verlängert, so dass zwei Balkone entstanden. Die quadratischen, 125x125 mm großen Säulen mit Verstärkungsträgern sind in Form eines X angeordnet und strategisch so verteilt, dass die Blickrichtung nicht unterbrochen wird. Im Inneren bildet ein Podium aus Massivholz den organischen Kontrapunkt zu dem Stahl, Glas und Beton. Es handelt sich vor allem um ein einfaches und effizientes Gebäude, in dem man das gesucht hat, was wirklich grundlegend für das Wohnen wichtig ist.

A thin glass screen divides the house from the street and the rear patio, whilst permitting adequate ventilation and lighting.

La membrane de verre isole la maison du bruit de la rue et du patio arrière, tout en permettant une ventilation et un éclairage adéquats.

Eine schmale Glasmembran trennt das Haus vom Lärm der Straße und dem Hinterhof und sorgt für eine ausgezeichnete Belüftung und Beleuchtung.

› Ground floor Rez-de-chaussée Erdgeschoss

› First floor Premier étage Erstes Obergeschoss

› Second floor Deuxième étage Zweites Obergeschoss

138 Barcom Avenue

In between a six-story commercial building and a row of single-level terraced houses, the shape of this plot forced the construction to be broken down into four distinct elements: one free-standing element and another, split in two, linked to the first by a shared corridor. The resulting L-shape homes on the ground floor form the base supporting a tiered volume jutting from an embedded transference structure. A transparent white glass stairwell next to the main entrance and a corridor on three levels leading to each home complete the complicated layout of this building. The 26-apartment complex contains seven different types of house, each with its own kitchen, washroom, study and storage space. The two homes on the top floor have skylights in the sloping roof, allowing plenty of natural light and ventilation to reach the bathroom, study and communal areas.

Situé entre un immeuble commercial de six étages et une rangée de maisons jumelles d'un étage, l'édifice, par la forme du terrain, se découpe en quatre éléments distincts : un qui est indépendant et l'autre divisé en deux, uni au premier par un passage commun. La disposition en L des chambres du niveau inférieur forme un podium sur lequel s'élève, en saillie, un volume échelonné depuis une structure de transfert encastrée. Une tour d'escalier de verre blanc translucide, contiguë à l'entrée principale, et un couloir sur trois niveaux accédant aux habitations, complètent cet édifice à la distribution compliquée. Ce complexe de 26 habitations est divisé en sept types différents, chacun disposant de cuisine, buanderie, penderie, studio et zones de rangement. Chacune des deux habitations supérieures possède une lucarne inclinée, permettant à la lumière d'entrer dans la salle de bains, le studio et le plan de l'étage central, tout en assurant la ventilation.

Da dieses Gebäude zwischen einem sechs-stöckigen Geschäftshaus und einer Serie von einstöckigen Reihenhäusern liegt, hat das Grundstück eine Form, die aus vier verschiedenen Elementen besteht. Die L-Form der Wohnungen im Untergeschoss formt ein Podium, auf dem sich eine überstehende, gestufte Masse auf einer eingebauten Struktur erhebt. Ein Treppenturm aus weißem, durchsichtigem Glas am Haupteingang und ein dreistöckiger Flur, in dem die Eingänge zu den Wohnungen liegen, vervollständigen dieses Gebäude, in dem es sehr schwierig war, Verbindungen zu schaffen. Es entstanden 26 Wohnungen, die sich in sieben verschiedene Typen unterteilen. Sie enthalten eine Küche, einen Waschraum, ein Kleiderzimmer, ein Atelier und Abstellräume. In den beiden oberen Wänden gibt es geneigte Dachfenster, durch die Licht und Luft in das Badezimmer, das Atelier und in das Zentrum der Wohnung gelangen.

A large portion of the façade incorporates aluminum screens for protection against sun and rain and for the provision of natural ventilation.

Une grande partie de la façade intègre l'aluminium pour la protéger du soleil et de la pluie et favoriser la ventilation naturelle.

Ein großer Teil der Fassade ist mit Aluminium verkleidet, das vor der Sonne und dem Regen schützt und die natürliche Belüftung begünstigt.

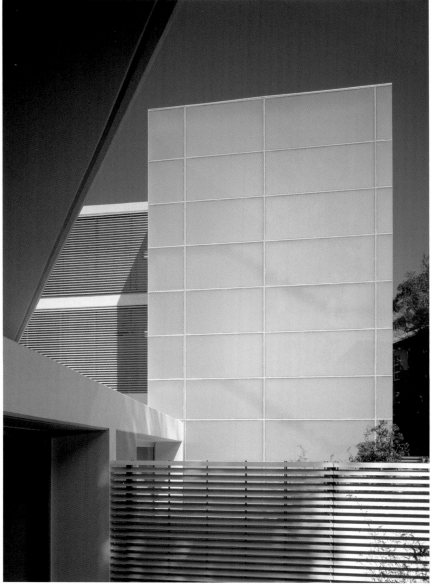

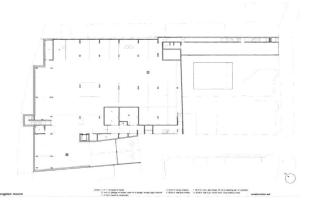

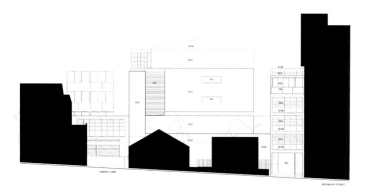

› Plan Plan Grundriss

› Elevation Élévation Aufriss

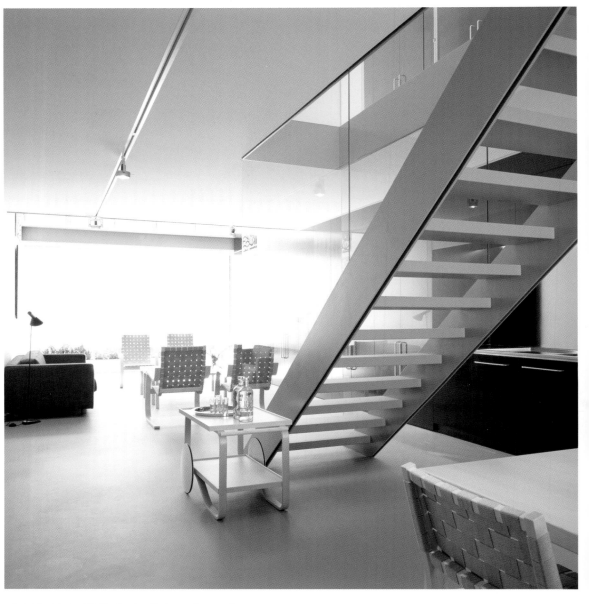

The various sections making up the whole building convey an overall sense of "joie de vivre", dynamism and space.

La présence de nombreux recoins confère à l'édifice une apparence gaie, imprégnée de dynamisme et d'une sensation d'espace.

Die Komposition der zahlreichen Winkel verleiht dem Gebäude ein frisches Aussehen: es wirkt dynamisch und groß.

White, Blue and Black
Blanc, bleu et noir
Weiß, Blau und Schwarz

The design for this house started from the following premise: the structure was to be painted white, the supporting elements black and the main pieces of furniture blue. This determined the interior configuration well before the plans were drawn up, guaranteeing a highly personalized interior, that would prevent everyday objects from losing their charm. Corridors with latticework on the ceilings and floors lead to the lower level and allow overhead light to flood the entire ground floor. This system also allows cool air to circulate in summertime. This architectural project uses extremely simple means—for example, the top floor design with alternate use of different light sources, such as overhead skylights and generous windows—to successfully forge a unique, coherent residence that is both functional and appealing.

Le design de cette maison part de l'idée suivante : une structure peinte en blanc, des éléments de soutien en noir et les principaux éléments du mobilier en bleu. La configuration des intérieurs était ainsi conçue à l'avance, même avant de tracer les plans, garantissant un intérieur personnalisé, exempt de toute banalisation d'objets quotidiens. A l'intérieur, les couloirs, dotés d'un caillebotis au plafond et au sol, communiquent entre eux et avec le niveau inférieur, laissant entrer la lumière du haut, qui pénètre dans tous les espaces du rez-de-chaussée. Grâce à ce système, l'air peut également circuler en été, garantissant fraîcheur et ambiance sèche. Le projet est un exercice architectural employant des moyens très simples -le design de l'étage supérieur et l'emplacement des sources de lumière, qu'elles viennent d'en haut ou par les grandes baies vitrées- pour réussir à créer une habitation très personnelle et harmonieuse, tout en étant fonctionnelle et agréable.

Die Gestaltung dieses Hauses ging von den folgenden Voraussetzungen aus: die Struktur sollte weiß, die stützenden Elemente schwarz und die wichtigsten Möbel blau sein. So wurde die Gestaltung der Innenräume bereits vorbestimmt, bevor überhaupt die Pläne gemacht wurden. Diese Tatsache garantierte eine persönliche Gestaltung der Räume, die nicht durch alltägliche Objekte banalisiert werden konnten. Die Flure sind mit dem Fachwerk an der Decke und der Boden mit der unteren Ebene verbunden. Sie lassen Licht von oben durchfallen, das in alle Räume im Erdgeschoss dringt. Dieses System lässt im Sommer auch die Luft zirkulieren. So sind die Räume kühl und trocken. Dieses Haus zeigt auf beispielhafte Weise architektonische Lösungen, bei denen sehr einfache Mittel eingesetzt wurden, wie z. B. die Gestaltung der oberen Etage und die Anordnung der Lichtquellen: das Licht fällt von oben oder durch große Fenster ein. So entstand eine sehr persönliche und durchgängige Wohnumgebung, die gleichzeitig funktionell und komfortabel ist.

The structure and walls are painted white, the supporting elements black and the main pieces of furniture blue.

La structure et la totalité des murs sont peintes en blanc, les éléments de soutien, en noir et les principaux éléments du mobilier en bleu.

Die Struktur ist weiß, die stützenden Elemente schwarz und die wichtigsten Möbel sind blau.

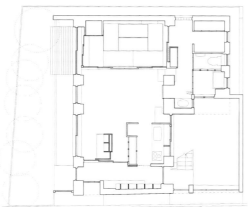

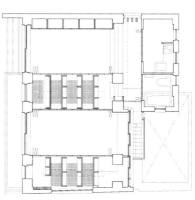

› Ground floor Rez-de-chaussée Erdgeschoss

› First floor Premier étage Erstes Obergeschoss

Residence in Valldoreix

Résidence à Valldoreix

Haus in Valldoreix

In this project, the client desired a home conceived on austere lines, with the exterior closely involved with the interior and communications between different areas playing a central role. The architect came up with a wall running parallel to the street, with one entrance for the garage and another for the garden. This wall bestows privacy on the property, sets up an east-west reference and defines spaces for the stairs and inner patio, which receives an abundance of sunlight and leads to a study and the guest bedroom. The first floor contains the everyday communal areas, arranged on a longitudinal plan in the form of a prism. The opening in the double-height dining room is wedged between the two blocks, separating them and casting light on the entire communicating area through the large window overlooking the patio.

Dans ce projet, le client désirait une habitation aux formes austères, où la relation avec l'extérieur et la communication entre les espaces étaient impératives. L'architecte a proposé de créer un mur longeant la rue avec un accès au garage et une entrée sur le terrain. Le mur confère au jardin un caractère privé, crée un axe est-ouest et définit un espace comprenant un escalier et un petit patio intérieur. Situé devant la maison, il reçoit en abondance la lumière solaire et s'ouvre sur un studio et une chambre d'amis. Le rez-de-chaussée accueille les zones d'activité quotidiennes, sous la forme d'un prisme longitudinal. L'ouverture sur la salle à manger à double hauteur se trouve entre les deux blocs, les isolant, et illumine toute la zone de communication grâce à la grande fenêtre avec vue sur le patio.

Der Kunde, der sich dieses Haus bauen ließ, wünschte sich schlichte Formen, bei denen die Beziehung zur Umgebung und die Verbindung zwischen den Räumen die wichtigste Rolle spielten. Der Architekt schuf eine Schiebewand, die parallel zur Straße verläuft und die einen Zugang zur Garage und auf das Grundstück schafft. Die Wand schirmt den Garten ab, schafft eine Ost-West-Achse und definiert den Raum, der eine Treppe und einen kleinen Innenhof enthält. In diesen kleinen Vorhof des Hauses fällt sehr viel Sonnenlicht ein. Er öffnet sich zu einem Atelier und einem Gästezimmer. Im Erdgeschoss liegen die Räume, die tagsüber genutzt werden und die Form eines länglichen Prismas haben. Die Öffnung zum Speisezimmer doppelter Höhe befindet sich zwischen den zwei Blöcken. So werden die Blöcke getrennt und durch das große Fenster mit Blick auf den Hof fällt Licht in den Durchgangsbereich.

The ground-floor living room receives natural light through the double-height window overlooking the garden.

La salle de séjour, située au rez-de-chaussée, reçoit la lumière naturelle par le biais de la fenêtre à double hauteur qui donne sur le jardin.

Das Wohnzimmer im Erdgeschoss erhält Tageslicht durch die Fenster doppelter Höhe, die zum Garten liegen.

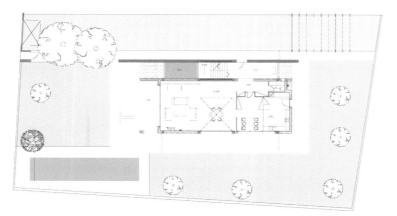

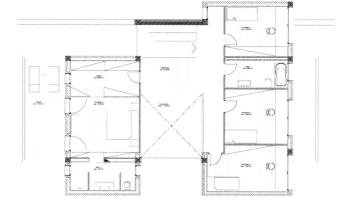

› Ground floor   Rez-de-chaussée   Erdgeschoss

› First floor   Premier étage   Erstes Obergeschoss

Inclined Residence
Maison inclinée
Geneigtes Haus

This unusual house offers an environmentally sound solution for a near-impossible terrain on a very steep, north-facing hillside. The house attempts to capture and preserve energy through its design: the gradient was calculated to accumulate heat in the winter and provide shade during the summer. During the hottest months, the lower floors enjoy cool shade and, because the roof extends beyond the top of the hill, it can also capture the rays of the low-lying winter sun. The interior is finished entirely in light wood, including the furniture, such as the table and fitted closets. A large opening to the north endows the house with spectacular views of the mountains.

Cette habitation particulière offre une solution respectant l'environnement sur un terrain impossible : un coteau très en pente, orienté nord. La maison essaie de capturer et de garder un certain dynamisme par le biais de son design : son inclinaison a été calculée pour accumuler la chaleur en hiver et fournir de l'ombre en été. Durant les mois les plus chauds, la zone du demi sous-sol bénéficie d'une réfrigération passive, grâce à la toiture qui s'étend au-delà de la cime de la colline, et, durant l'hiver, profite de la chaleur due à l'inclinaison des rayons de soleil. Les finitions intérieures sont exclusivement réalisées en bois clair, ainsi que les revêtements des meubles, à l'instar de la table ou des armoires encastrées. Grâce à une grande ouverture au nord, l'habitation bénéficie d'une vue spectaculaire sur les montagnes.

Dieses außergewöhnliche Haus geht sehr respektvoll mit der Umgebung um. Es steht auf einem Grundstück, das als nicht bebaubar erscheinen mag: einem sehr abschüssigen Nordhang. Das Haus versucht die Energie durch seine Gestaltung einzufangen und zu erhalten. Die Neigung wurde so berechnet, dass im Winter Wärme gespeichert und im Sommer Schatten gespendet wird. In den heißen Monaten besitzt das Halbsouterrain eine passive Kühlung, die durch ein Dach erreicht wird, das sich über den Gipfel des Hügels erstreckt. Im Winter werden die schräg einfallenden Strahlen der tiefstehenden Wintersonne ausgenutzt. Im Inneren wurde ausschließlich helles Holz für die Oberflächen benutzt, ebenso für die Möbel, den Tisch und die eingebauten Schränke. Durch eine große Öffnung im Norden hat man von dem Haus aus einen wundervollen Blick auf die umliegenden Berge.

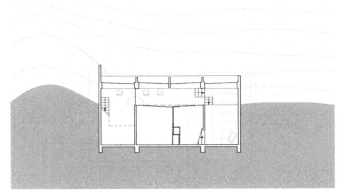

› Ground floor Rez-de-chaussée Erdgeschoss

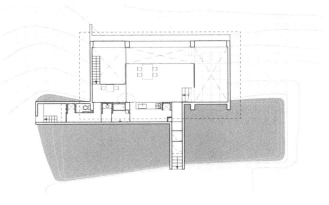

› First floor Premier étage Erstes Obergeschoss

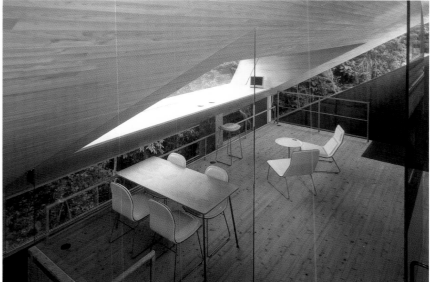

A large opening to the north is integrated into the vertical walls to provide spectacular views of the mountains.

Une grande ouverture orientée nord est intégrée dans les murs verticaux, offrant des vues sur les montagnes.

Eine große Öffnung nach Norden in den senkrechten Wänden öffnet den Blick auf die Berge.

Slice Residence

Maison Slice

Haus Slice

This house, built on a site that became empty after the construction of a new road, is characterized by its sliced outline. The design evokes the modern, minimalist architecture of Brazil, complemented by a new element, in the form of complex prismatic geometry, creating a series of distinctive settings in the interior. The central patio creates a microclimate, allowing the house to be completely open during the summer months. Distorted spaces, sloping angles and innovative perspectives are the distinguishing features of this design. The swimming pool on the ground floor has been integrated into the living area and acts as a filter of light, sending rippled reflections from the water surface.

Cette habitation, construite sur un terrain laissé à l'abandon depuis la création d'une nouvelle route, revêt l'aspect d'une tranche (slice). Le projet évoque l'architecture brésilienne moderne et minimaliste, agrémentée d'un nouvel élément qui se traduit par une géométrie prismatique complexe, créant une série d'impressions spéciales à l'intérieur. Un patio situé au centre de l'édifice génère un microclimat, permettant d'ouvrir entièrement la maison en été. Espaces déformés, angles inclinés et perspectives innovantes sont les traits caractéristiques qui définissent ce design. La structure de la piscine, située au rez-de-chaussée, s'intègre à la salle de séjour et filtre la lumière du jour, qui fait scintiller l'eau.

Dieses Haus steht auf einem Grundstück, das nach dem Erschließen einer neuen Straße unbenutzt blieb und die Form einer Schnitte (slice) hat. Die Planung ist von der modernen, minimalistischen Architektur Brasiliens beeinflusst, der mit der komplexen prismatischen Geometrie ein neues Element hinzugefügt wurde, durch das eine Reihe von räumlichen Illusionen im Inneren entsteht. Durch einen Hof in der Mitte des Gebäudes wird ein Mikroklima geschaffen, so dass man das Haus im Sommer vollständig öffnen kann. Verformte Räume, geneigte Winkel und innovative Perspektiven sind die typischen Züge der Gestaltung. Die Struktur des Swimmingpools im Erdgeschoss wurde in das Wohnzimmer integriert und dient als Filter für das Tageslicht. Das Licht, das die gekräuselte Oberfläche des Wassers durchquert, lässt interessante Effekte entstehen.

The swimming pool structure is a part of the living room and serves to filter the sunlight penetrating inside.

La structure de la piscine est intégrée à la salle de séjour et filtre la lumière du jour.

Die Struktur des Swimmingpools wurde in das Wohnzimmer integriert und dient als Filter für das Tageslicht.

 › Section Section Schnitt

 › Elevation Élévation Aufriss

Distorted spaces, sloping angles and innovative perspectives characterise this design.

Espaces déformés, angles inclinés et perspectives innovatrices, définissent le design.

Verformte Räume, geneigte Winkel und innovative Perspektiven sind die typischen Gestaltungsmerkmale.

Residence in Majorca

Maison à Majorque

Residenz auf Mallorca

Near the sea shore but at the same time surrounded by meadows, this house enjoys magnificent views of the surroundings. The structure is set upon a concrete base which unites the interior and exterior of the house. The entrance is distinguished by a wooden floor and a small corridor with a concrete roof. The whole composition, simple and linear, is well-defined; the rooms are distinguished and differentiated by their forms and materials. The living-room and dining-room areas are situated on the lower floor, which is focused toward the façade, the long rectangular swimming pool and the outdoor terrace. The concrete wall extends around one corner of the property, framing a large landscaped patio, laid with concrete tiles and interspersed with trees and lawn.

Proche de la mer, mais entourée à la fois d'une prairie, cette maison jouit de vues magnifiques sur les environs. La structure se définit par une base de béton qui enveloppe l'intérieur et l'extérieur. L'entrée est caractérisée par un plancher en bois et par un petit passage couvert d'un toit de béton. Toute la composition, sobre et linéaire, est bien définie. Formes et matériaux caractérisent et différencient les chambres. Les zones du salon et de la salle à manger sont situées au rez-de-chaussée tourné vers la façade, la longue piscine rectangulaire et la terrasse extérieure. Le mur de béton entoure un angle du terrain, encadrant un grand patio paysagé, recouvert de dalles de béton et agrémenté d'arbres et de gazon.

Dieses Haus liegt in der Nähe des Meeres und ist von einer Wiese umgeben, von der man einen wundervollen Blick auf die Umgebung hat. Die Struktur besteht aus einer Grundlage aus Beton, die das Innere und Äußere umgibt. Der Holzboden markiert den Eingang quer durch einen Flur, der mit einem Dach aus Beton gedeckt ist. Die gesamte Kombination, die einfach und linear ist, ist gut definiert. Die Zimmer werden durch ihre Formen und Materialien voneinander unterschieden und gekennzeichnet. Die Bereiche des Wohn- und Speisezimmers befinden sich im Erdgeschoss, wo Fenster in der Fassade den Blick auf den langen rechteckigen Swimmingpool und die Terrasse freigeben. Die Betonwand, die eine Ecke des Geländes umgibt, umrahmt den großen, begrünten Hof, der mit Betonplatten überdacht und mit Bäumen und Rasen bepflanzt ist.

The windows, doors and walls act as counterweights maintaining the balance of the composition.

Les fenêtres, portes et murs, faisant contrepoids, équilibrent la composition.

Die Fenster, Türen und Wände dienen als Gegengewicht, so dass die Komposition ihr Gleichgewicht hält.

The openings in the concrete walls frame the magnificent views of the surroundings.

Les ouvertures dans les murs de béton encadrent le paysage extérieur, entouré de végétation.

Die Öffnungen in den Betonwänden umrahmen die üppige Landschaft der Umgebung.

Residence in Ibaraki
Maison à Ibaraki
Haus in Ibaraki

Surrounded by traditional houses, this rather unconventional home comprises two rectangular volumes. Facing east, the sloping facades of the upper volume mimic a typical pitched roof, whilst simultaneously introducing novelty into the structure. By day, the horizon is reflected in the main façade; by night, the inside of the building shines like a lighthouse, whilst the contrasting materials and finishes, such as polished steel and textured stone, create a modern, dynamic effect. The play of contrasts is repeated inside: the texture of the wooden floors is set off by the roughness of the stone walls. Both stories are completely open spaces that take advantage of the light entering through the enormous windows to give the impression of boundless freedom.

Entourée de maisons traditionnelles, cette habitation, à la structure peu conventionnelle, est formée de deux volumes rectangulaires. Orientées à l'est, les façades en biais du volume supérieur imitent la toiture typique à deux pentes tout en bouleversant sa structure en transformant l'arête centrale en élément plat. De jour, l'horizon se reflète dans la façade principale. De nuit, l'intérieur de l'habitation s'illumine, à l'instar d'un phare, tandis que le contraste entre les différents matériaux et finitions, comme l'acier poli et la roche structurée, génère un effet moderne et dynamique. A l'intérieur, le jeu de contrastes se répète : la texture des parquets se découpe sur la surface rugueuse des murs de pierre. Les deux étages sont deux espaces complètement ouverts qui, profitant de la lumière qui pénètre par les immenses baies vitrées, donnent l'impression d'être d'une amplitude infinie.

Dieses von traditionellen Häusern umgebene Gebäude besitzt eine sehr unkonventionelle Struktur aus zwei rechteckigen Formen. Die nach Osten weisende, schräg geschnittene Fassade der oberen Form ahmt ein typisches Satteldach nach, während sie gleichzeitig eine neue Struktur einführt, indem sie die mittlere Kante in ein flaches Element verwandelt. Tagsüber spiegelt sich der Horizont an der Hauptfassade wider, nachts ist das Innere des Hauses wie ein Leuchtturm beleuchtet. Durch den Kontrast zwischen den verschiedenen Materialien und Oberflächen, wie polierter Stahl und Naturstein, wirkt das Gesamtbild modern und dynamisch. Im Inneren wiederholt sich dieses Spiel mit den Gegensätzen: die Textur der Holzböden zeichnet sich vor der rauhen Oberfläche der Steinwände ab. Die beiden Etagen sind völlig offene Räume, in die reichlich Licht aus den riesigen Fenstern fällt, so dass sie fast unendlich wirken.

The contrast between the materials and finishes, such as polished steel and textured stone, creates a modern, dynamic effect.

Le contraste entre les différents matériaux et finis, à l'instar de l'acier poli et de la roche rugueuse, engendre un effet moderne et dynamique.

Der Kontrast zwischen den verschiedenen Materialien und Oberflächen, wie poliertem Stahl und Naturstein mit rauer Oberfläche, wirkt sehr modern und dynamisch.

By day, the horizon is reflected in the main façade; by night, the inside of the building shines like a beacon.

De jour, l'horizon se reflète dans la façade principale. De nuit, l'intérieur de l'habitation est éclairé comme un phare.

Tagsüber spiegelt sich der Horizont an der Hauptfassade, nachts ist das Innere des Hauses wie ein Leuchtturm beleuchtet.

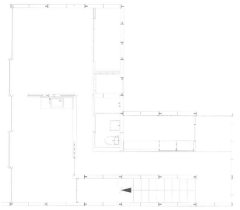

› First floor Premier étage Erstes Obergeschoss

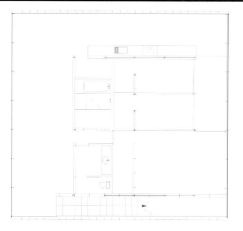

› Second floor Deuxième étage Zweites Obergeschoss

House in Vandoeuvres

Maison à Vandoeuvres

Haus in Vandoeuvres

The structure for this new house, which also accommodates a doctor's surgery, strikes up a contrast with the traditional style of the main building, dating from the seventies. Large skylights flood the interior with sunlight, while the opaque glass ensures the necessary degree of privacy. The windows, fitted with filters to minimize the amount of sunlight penetrating inside and prevent overheating, are placed on either side of the sloping ceiling, like pieces of a jigsaw, to mitigate the claustrophobic impression created by an exterior structure made entirely of concrete. At night, a lighting system close to the windows endows the garden with the atmosphere of an illuminated swimming pool, producing an optical effect similar to that of a television in a dark room.

La nouvelle structure de cette maison, réunissant à la fois habitation et cabinet médical, contraste avec le style traditionnel de l'édifice principal construit dans les années soixante-dix. Les grandes lucarnes du toit inondent l'espace de la lumière naturelle et l'opacité du verre garantie l'intimité nécessaire à un cabinet de consultations. Les fenêtres sont équipées de filtres pour diminuer l'impact de la lumière solaire et les risques de surchauffe de l'intérieur. Sur le plan esthétique, les fenêtres ont été insérées sur des cotés opposés du toit, à l'instar des pièces d'un puzzle, pour atténuer l'impression de fermeture engendrée par une structure extérieure entièrement en ciment. De nuit, un système d'éclairage situé près des fenêtres s'allume, conférant au jardin l'ambiance nocturne d'une piscine éclairée, produisant un effet optique semble à celui d'une télévision dans une pièce obscure.

Die neue Struktur dieses Hauses, in dem außer eine Wohnung auch eine Arztpraxis untergebracht ist, steht zu dem traditionellen Stil des Hauptgebäudes aus den Siebzigerjahren im Gegensatz. Die großen Dachfenster lassen reichlich Licht in den Raum einfallen und das undurchsichtige Glas sorgt für die notwendige Privatsphäre in der Arztpraxis. Die Fenster sind mit Filtern ausgestattet, die gegen das Sonnenlicht abschirmen und vermeiden, dass es zu warm wird. Sie wurden auf zwei gegenüberliegenden Seiten in der Decke eingebaut, so als ob es sich um Teile eines Puzzles handelte. Damit öffnete man auch gleichzeitig die Außenstruktur, die vollständig aus Zement besteht. Nachts schalten sich Beleuchtungskörper in der Nähe der Fenster ein, die im Garten eine nächtliche Landschaft mit einem beleuchteten Swimmingpool schaffen, der so hypnotisch wirkt wie ein Fernseher in einem dunklen Raum.

347

A large skylight made of opaque glass filters sunlight throughout the interior, while ensuring the necessary degree of privacy.

La grande lucarne de verre opaque diffuse la lumière naturelle à tout l'espace, tout en lui conférant l'intimité nécessaire.

Das große gläserne Dachfenster lässt Tageslicht in den gesamten Raum fallen. Das undurchsichtige Glas sorgt gleichzeitig für die nötige Intimsphäre.

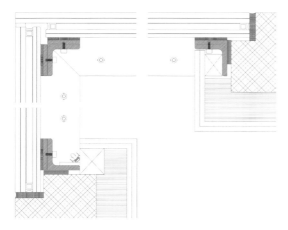

› Plan Plan Grundriss

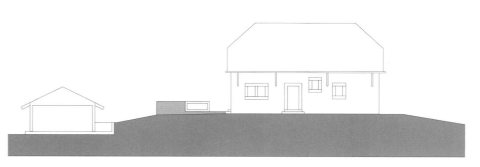

› Elevation Élévation Aufriss

Böhler-Tembl Residence

Maison Böhler-Tembl

Haus Böhler-Tembl

This two-story house, situated in the eastern part of the Rhine valley, has glass façades and a concrete structure resting on a wooden walkway facing an orchard. Two projecting wings in the concrete structure, one at the back of the house and the other on the side, provide space for a garage and a terrace. The interior is designed according to strictly minimalist concepts, characterized by straight parallel lines and lighting effects. A fireplace of contemporary design in the living room acts as a functional element, as well as being decorative. A balcony projecting from the concrete construction provides shade on the terrace of the ground floor, the setting for the bedrooms and the bathrooms.

Cette maison à deux étages, située à l'est de la vallée du Rhin, possède des façades en verre et une structure de béton reposant sur une passerelle de bois orientée vers une plantation d'arbres fruitiers. Les extensions en saillie de la structure de béton, une à l'arrière de l'habitation et l'autre sur un côté, créent un garage et une terrasse. L'espace intérieur est dessiné selon un concept très minimaliste, caractérisé par les lignes droites et parallèles et par l'utilisation des effets de lumière. Dans la salle de séjour, une cheminée au design contemporain, est à la fois fonctionnelle et décorative. Un balcon surplombant la structure de béton offre de l'ombre à la terrasse du dernier étage qui accueille les chambres à coucher et les salles de bains.

Dieses zweistöckige Haus im Rheintal hat verglaste Fassaden und eine Betonstruktur, die auf einem Holzsteg ruht und in Richtung einer Obstbaumpflanzung weist. Zwei Verlängerungen auf einem Vorsprung der Betonstruktur, eine hinten und eine auf der Seite, schaffen Platz für eine Garage und eine Terrasse. Das Innere des Hauses ist nach einem stark minimalistischen Konzept entworfen, in dem gerade und parallele Linien vorherrschen und das Licht benutzt wird, um bestimmte Effekte zu erzielen. Ein moderner Kamin im Wohnzimmer ist gleichzeitig ein funktionelles und dekoratives Element. Ein Balkon, der über die Betonstruktur hinaussteht, wirft Schatten auf die Terrasse des letzten Stockwerks, in dem die Schlafzimmer und die Badezimmer liegen.

Natural light streams through the large glass doors, illuminating the whole ground floor and providing panoramic views of the surrounding landscape.

La lumière naturelle entre par les grandes portes de verre, illuminant tout le rez-de-chaussée, ce qui permet d'obtenir une vue panoramique sur le paysage environnant.

Das Tageslicht fällt durch die großen Glastüren ein und erhellt das gesamte Erdgeschoss. Gleichzeitig hat man einen wundervollen Blick auf die umgebende Landschaft.

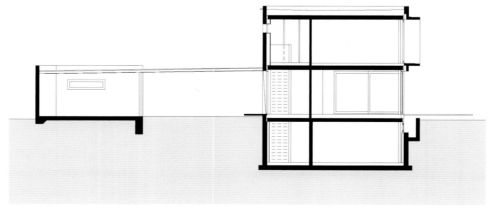

› Section Section Schnitt

Emery Residence
Résidence Emery
Haus Emery

Located on an extremely steep hillside, this project stands out for its bold design, composed of rectilinear structures projecting toward the sea. The upper volume juts out slightly above the surrounding trees, giving the impression of floating in the air. The simple lines of the structure, made of a steel frame supporting concrete blocks, are enhanced by cunning details like the sloping chimney stack or the division of the main unit into two halves. The interior plasterwork has been painted white, and wood-clad boxes serve as furniture as well as dividing screens or closets in this otherwise completely open space.

Ce projet, situé sur le flanc d'une colline très pentue, frappe par son design audacieux, composé de structures rectilignes qui se projettent vers la mer. Le volume supérieur, un peu plus grand que les arbres qui l'entourent, déborde en saillie, donnant l'impression de flotter dans l'air. La simplicité de la structure, formée par un cadre d'acier soutenant les blocs de béton, est enrichie par les détails subtils comme la cheminée oblique ou la division de l'unité principale en deux sections. L'intérieur est badigeonné de blanc et des boites, revêtues de plaques de bois, servent tantôt de mobilier, de cloisons ou d'armoires dans cet espace complètement ouvert.

Dieses Haus auf einem sehr steilen Hang zeichnet sich durch sein gewagtes Design aus. Die geradlinigen Strukturen weisen in Richtung Meer. Die obere Form ist etwas höher als die Bäume, die sie umgeben und sie formt einen Vorsprung, der den Eindruck entstehen lässt, dass sie in der Luft schwebt. Die einfache Struktur, bestehend aus einem Stahlrahmen, der die Zementblöcke hält, wird durch feine Details wie den schrägen Kamin oder die Aufteilung des Hauptkörpers in zwei Sektionen bereichert. Der Putz im Inneren wurde weiß gestrichen und mit Holzfurnier verkleidete Kisten dienen als Möbel, als Raumteiler und als Schränke in diesem völlig offenen Raum.

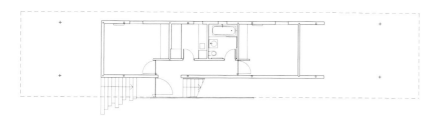

› Ground floor Rez-de-chaussée Erdgeschoss

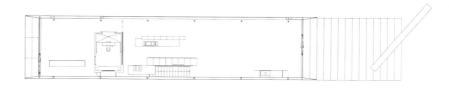

› First floor Premier étage Erstes Obergeschoss

Misonou House
Maison Misonou
Haus Misonou

When contemplating the design of this structure, the client sought above all to create a close relationship between the home and the natural surroundings. The absence of an opaque facade on the ground floor removed the traditional barrier between interior and exterior, creating a space much greater than that of a typical façade. In the absence of corner columns, the second floor seems to be suspended from above. A cube-shape volume resting on a glass wall contains an upper level that seems to float above the ground. Inside, a single open space feels like an extension of the landscape, rather than rooms within a building. Radiant underfloor heating was installed to maintain a constant temperature, and a surface made entirely of concrete passively makes use of solar energy.

Le client, à l'origine du design de cette structure, voulait surtout créer une étroite relation entre l'habitation et l'environnement naturel. L'absence de façade opaque au niveau inférieur efface la séparation traditionnelle entre l'intérieur et l'extérieur et crée un espace plus grand que dans le cas d'une façade classique. Les colonnes d'angle éliminées, créent l'illusion de suspension du niveau par le haut. La forme cubique sur ce mur de verre dispose d'un deuxième niveau qui semble flotter au-dessus du rez-de-chaussée. A l'intérieur, une pièce unique, sans aucune espèce de division, se définit comme un espace ouvert qui ressemble davantage à une extension du paysage qu'à l'intérieur d'un édifice. Pour garder une température constante, le sol est à chaleur radiante, et il y a une surface tout en ciment utilisant passivement l'énergie solaire.

Die wichtigste Bedingung des Kunden, und somit fundamental für den Entwurf der Anlage, war die enge Verbidung zwischen dem Wohnraum und der Natur. Da es im Untergeschoss keine undurchsichtige Fassade gibt, die den Blick versperrt, gibt es auch diese typische Trennung zwischen innen und außen nicht. Deshalb wirkt der Raum viel größer als der, der sich hinter einer klassischen Fassade befindet. Die Säulen an den Ecken wurden entfernt und es entstand der Eindruck, dass die darüberliegende Ebene aufgehängt ist. Die kubische Form über der Glaswand enthält die zweite Ebene, die über dem Erdgeschoss zu schweben scheint. Im Inneren gibt es nur einen einzigen Raum ohne jegliche Unterteilung: ein offener Raum, der eher einer Fortsetzung der Landschaft als dem Inneren eines Gebäudes gleicht. Um die Temperatur konstant zu halten, installierte man eine Fußbodenheizung und eine durchgehende Zementfläche, durch die die Sonnenenergie passiv ausgenutzt wird.

A cube-shape volume resting on a glass wall contains an upper level that seems to float above the ground.

La structure cubique au-dessus des murs de verre englobe le second niveau et semble flotter sur le terrain.

Die kubische Struktur über den Glaswänden enthält eine zweite Etage, die über dem Grundstück zu schweben scheint.

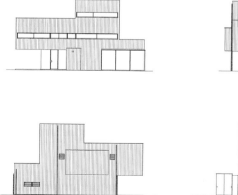

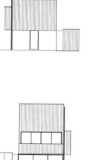

› Plan Plan Grundriss

› Elevations Élévations Aufrisse

House in Dornbirn
Maison à Dornbirn
Haus in Dornbirn

In order to gain full benefit of the position and the natural light, the architect situated this house on the edge of a hill. The three-story structure has its lowest floor concealed beneath the ground; the other two floors are arranged on different levels, so that a balcony is created at the rear. The main façade, which faces west, offers the opportunity to enjoy spectacular sunsets. Both façades—east and west—are glazed, whilst the north and south sides are completely blind, with the exception of two medium-sized windows. Coated with gray-green paint, the brick wall gives off sparkling reflections when its pigments are struck by the sun's rays. The use of pale wood and polished concrete inside the house creates a warm and homely atmosphere that contrasts with the cold bleakness outside.

Pour exploiter les vues dues à l'emplacement et à la lumière naturelle, l'architecte a situé cette maison au bord d'une pente. La structure des trois étages cache le niveau inférieur, enterré, les deux autres sont distribués de manière échelonnée, formant un balcon sur la partie arrière. La façade principale, orientée ouest, permet de jouir de superbes couchers de soleil. Les façades ouest et est sont toutes deux revêtues de verre, tandis que les côtés nord et sud sont complètement fermés, à l'exception de deux fenêtres de format moyen. Peint dans un mélange de couleur minérale gris verdâtre, le mur en brique est doté de pigments irradiant des reflets iridescents quand ils entrent en contact avec les rayons du soleil. A l'intérieur, le bois aux tons clairs et le béton poli créent une ambiance chaude et accueillante, contrastant avec l'extérieur froid et brut.

Um den Blick auf die Umgebung und das Tageslicht wirklich zu nutzen, stellte der Architekt dieses Haus fast an den Rand des Hangs. Die Struktur aus drei Stockwerken versteckt das Untergeschoss unterirdisch, und die beiden anderen Etagen sind stufenförmig angeordnet, so dass hinten ein Balkon entstanden ist. Die Hauptfassade liegt Richtung Westen, so dass man von innen die wundervollen Sonnenuntergänge genießen kann. Die Ost- und Westfassade sind mit Glas verkleidet, während die Fassaden nach Norden und Süden, bis auf zwei mittelgroße Fenster, vollständig geschlossen sind. Das Haus ist mit einer Pigmentfarbe in einem grünlichen Grau gestrichen, die Wand ist aus Ziegelstein, dessen Pigmente schillernde Reflexe werfen, wenn die Sonnenstrahlen darauf fallen. Im Inneren wurde helles Holz und polierter Beton verwendet, so dass eine warme und einladende Atmosphäre entsteht, die einen Gegensatz zu dem kalten und strengen Anblick von außen bildet.

The perfect placement of the structure and large glazed surfaces allow light to be distributed uniformly and abundantly throughout the house.

L'orientation parfaite de la structure et des grands panneaux de verre permet une distribution uniforme et abondante de la lumière à travers toute la maison.

Die gelungene Ausrichtung der Struktur und die großen Glasscheiben ermöglichen eine gleichmäßige und großzügige Verteilung des Lichtes im ganzen Haus.

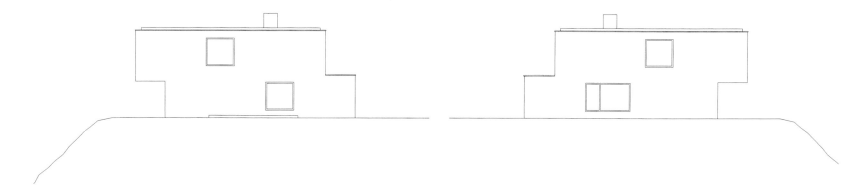

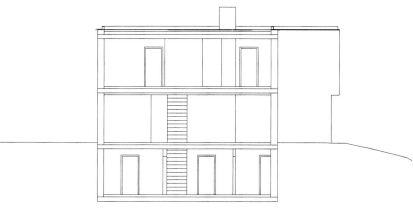

› Cross section   Section transversale   Querschnitt

4 x 4 House

Maison 4 x 4

Haus 4 x 4

This house on the sea shore faces toward Awaji Island, which was the epicentre of the 1995 Hanshin earthquake. The simple and straight-lined structure is formed from cube-shape components placed one on top of the other. The façade is made of concrete, which retains its original color and harmonizes with the natural colors of the surrounding country-side, such as the beach and the sea. The house, which takes its name from the four-square-metre plot upon which it rests, rises vertically to offer impressive panoramic views. The contemporary interior design combines modern furniture, such as the Rietveld Zig Zag chair, with traditional Japanese seats. The flooring is made of pale timber, which reflects the light entering during the day.

Cette maison, située au bord de la mer, est tournée vers l'île Awaji, épicentre du grand tremblement de terre de Hanshin en 1995. La simple structure aux lignes droites est constituée d'éléments cubiques superposés l'un au-dessus de l'autre. La façade est en béton, conservant sa couleur originale en harmonie avec les couleurs naturelles du paysage des alentours comme la plage et la mer. L'habitation, dont le nom vient des quatre mètres carrés sur lesquels elle repose, s'élève à la verticale pour offrir une impressionnante vue panoramique sur le paysage. Le design de cet intérieur contemporain associe au mobilier moderne, à l'instar du fauteuil Zig Zag de Rietveld, des sièges japonais traditionnels. Le sol est en bois clair, reflétant la lumière du jour.

Dieses Haus liegt am Meer mit Blick auf die Insel Awaji, die das Epizentrum des großen Erdbebens von Hanshin 1995 war. Die einfache Struktur mit geraden Linien besteht aus übereinander liegenden, kubischen Elementen. Die Fassade ist aus Beton in seiner Originalfarbe, die gut zu den Farben der umliegenden Landschaft, zum Strand und zum Meer passt. Dieses Haus, das seinen Namen den vier Quadratmetern Grundfläche verdankt, auf denen es errichtet wurde, erhebt sich vertikal, so dass man den beeindruckenden Blick auf die Landschaft ausnutzen konnte. Im Inneren wurden moderne Möbel wie der Zick-zack-Stuhl von Rietveld mit klassischen japanischen Stühlen kombiniert. Der Boden ist aus hellem Holz, das das Tageslicht reflektiert.

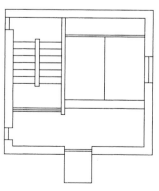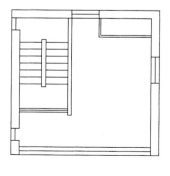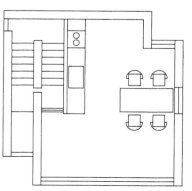

› Plans Plans Grundrisse

This contemporary interior design combines modern furniture, such as the Rietveld Zig Zag chair, with traditional Japanese seats.

Le design de cet intérieur contemporain allie le mobilier moderne, à l'instar de la chaise Zig Zag de Rietveld, à des chaises japonaises traditionnelles.

Im Inneren wurden moderne Möbel wie der Zick-zack-Stuhl von Rietveld mit klassischen japanischen Stühlen kombiniert.

Photo Credits   Crédits photographiques   Fotonachweis